Degree Analyses:
Dwadashamsas and Deeper Meanings

Degree Analyses:
Dwadashamsas and Deeper Meanings

John Sandbach

Seek-It Publishing   P.O. Box 1074   Birmingham, Michigan 48012

This book is dedicated to
Antoinette Sandbach

AUTHOR'S PREFACE

This book was originally written in January of 1974, after nearly one year of intensive research. At the time, I had been a practicioner of astrology for eight years. During the writing of this book, I referred to over 80 charts — some were of people close to me, and some of famous personalities whom I felt in tune with.

The research that went into this work was of an analytic, yet subjective nature. Although I rationally and logically checked all of the ideas presented herein, the core of the material is of an inspirational nature. I have attempted to communicate the "feel" of each dwadashamsa, rather than to relate a dry, statistical exposition.

It seems to me that astrology is once more moving towards a "feeling" discipline. Although I believe objective research is valid, I also believe that much more is necessary for a well-rounded astrology. The stellar art needs both the thinking and the feeling — or intuitive — mind.

This book may be used most effectively as a reference text. The short essays on each dwad are not intended as a final word on the subject. Rather, they are meant to act as a "trigger" in the reader, a "sensing" for the understanding of the subtle colorations of sign blendings. *One must always take into account the particular planet appearing in the dwad* (should there be one), *as this adds yet another colortone to these sign blendings.*

The bull-headed Minotaur is Taurus, symbolizing *integration*. The astrological wheel is a labyrinth wherein lurks this hidden integration. Just as Jason found his way through the labyrinth by use of a thread, so too is this book a thread — a "line of thinking" one may use in finding the way through effective horoscope delineation.

Do not take these interpretations only at face value. Apply what you have already grasped about the signs, and use this book as an aid in penetrating more deeply into astrological meanings.

John Sandbach
March, 1978

TABLE OF CONTENTS

FORWARD
SYSTEMS OF DWADASHAMSAS

Dwadashamsas (or, as astrologer Charles Trudell states: "affectionately known as dwads"), are a very little understood branch of astrology. Even the history, or origin, of the concept of dwads seems unknown, though most writers on the subject attribute it to the ancient astrologers of India. Indeed the subject of dwadashamsas appears quite significant in the practice of Hindu Astrology,[1] as do other methods of sign division, where it is an important factor in the art of prognosticating events in a native's life.

The Westernized version of dwadashamsas has so far been used as a means of obtaining further insight into basic characteristics in a natal sense, as opposed to a prognosticative expression. It is the belief of many astrologers in the Western Hemisphere that within each sign of the zodiac, there appears to be different natures of expression and hence influence. For example, the inherent nature of the early degrees of a sign like Taurus seem quite unlike the later degrees of Taurus. Many astrologers would suggest this is so because of the cuspal influence, wherein the earlier degrees of a sign "carry over" qualities from the preceding sign (i.e. early Taurus would have Aries qualities), and the later degrees would assume characteristics of the following sign (i.e. late Taurus would possess characteristics of Gemini). Still other astrologers notice additional differences within a sign than merely the beginning and end segments, that throughout each sign certain characteristics or tendencies stand out — tendencies that are not so appar-

1

ent in the rest of that sign, let alone the rest of the zodiac. Astrologers like Charles Carter[2] and Maurice Wemyss[3] have gone so far as to demonstrate that certain and specific degrees of a zodiac sign — and not the entirety of the sign itself — appear in the charts of individuals who share the same vocation, hobby, bodily weaknesses and ailments, and psychological dispositions.

The idea that each zodiac sign contains within it several slightly different expressions — that a sign does not express the same specific qualities throughout its 30 degrees — is thus not a new idea. In fact, several books have been written which delineate every single degree of the zodiac. Some of these accounts have been via psychic observation, some through personal observation and research via trial and error methods, and some even through philosophical — numerological justifications.

Of all the techniques and methods presented in sign division and degree analyses, the concept of the dwadashamsa seems most logically based upon astrological theory. It seems "to fit" the most neatly in answering the question: "Why are there differences of expression within the same sign of the zodiac?"

The concept of dwadashamsas states that within each sign of the zodiac appears the modification influence of every other sign. Or, in a sense, that within the whole of a sign appears all of the parts — or signs — to which the signs themselves make up a greater whole. Therefore within the sign of Gemini, for instance, one will find that every other sign of the zodiac — in addition to Gemini — will have its particular area of modification to some degree.

The reason dwadashamsas "fit" so neatly is because every 30 degree sign can be divided by 2½ degrees exactly 12 times. Since 12 is the number of signs in the entire zodiac, every zodiac sign will have a sub-rulership over a particular 2½ degree segment within every sign. For example, within the sign of Aquarius, there are 12 divisions of 2½ degrees each. Each of these 12 divisions can then be assigned a different zodiac sign, and within the entire 30 degrees, every one of the 12 signs has its own sub-rulership. These 2½ degree sub-rulerships within each sign are known as the dwadashamsas of that sign.

The interpretation, or meaning, given to each dwadashamsa is a result of combining the primary sign itself with the modifying influence of the dwadashamsa's sign. For instance, the Sagittarius dwadashamsa of the sign Aquarius would have an influence of the nature of combining Sagittarius to the basic expression of Aquarius (i.e. philosophic original-ity, uniqueness in teaching others, friendship, or pos-sibly even fanaticism in thought and over-estimation of Man's virtues).

Though most astrologers are united in the attitude that different segments of a given sign exert slightly different characteristics, there has been to date no standard method of determining what — and where — those characteristics are. In the relatively unre-searched field of dwadashamsas, we notice at least four different approaches used in identifying- and hence interpretating- these 2½ degree segments of each sign. This book by John Sandbach is one of the more origi-nal and unique methods, and even as he states, it is not the final word in this study. And as I am certain he

3

recognizes, the method outlined in this book is not the method adopted by most astrologers who use dwadashamsas in their studies. Yet — as so often is the case in the study of astrology — we must continue to ask ourself the question when any new method is presented to us: "Does It Work?" Although I am but one independent tester of Sandbach's material, I can state confidently that my experience has borne out that his interpretation of the dwadashamsas has worked time and time again — much more profoundly than any other work I have used on the subject to date. And that is not to say that the other systems do not work — for they do — but Sandbach's interpretations cut far more deeply into the nature and motivation of an individual than I would have thought possible simply through degree analysis.

OTHER SYSTEMS

As stated, there are at least four ways of determining dwadashamsas. That means there are also at least four different ways to interpret each 2½ degree segment of a zodiac sign, depending on which method one uses. These four methods will be presented here, and the reader is encouraged to experiement with all four and see for him/herself which works most accurately. Since no name has been given to these different methods, I have decided to arbitrarily name them myself as a means of telling them apart from one another.

THE COMMON METHOD

The *common method* assumes that the first 2½ degrees of <u>any</u> sign is sub-ruled by Aries, the first sign of the zodiac. The second 2½ degrees of <u>every</u> sign is identified as the Taurus dwad, the next by the Gemini dwad, and so on until the last 2½ degrees, which are sub-ruled by Pisces.

The idea behind this method is that the first dwadashamsa of any sign represents a beginning experience, a new expression, which are the symbolical characteristics of Aries. Furthermore, Pisces represents the end, or the final completion of any effort, and therefore should have sub-rulership over the last degrees of any sign.

In the practice of astrology, we see this idea has merit. For example, in the study of secondary progressions, we notice that when a planet (particularly the progressed Sun or Moon) enters a new sign, it does in fact correspond with new conditions, new attitudes — and hence behavioral expressions — in the native's life. Matters begin to take on a new form, and there is the feeling of anticipation and excitment within the individual when a planet enters a new sign by progression.

Correlations are also noticed as a planet prepares to progress out of a sign. Matters in an individual's life seem to come to an end, and the attitude is often one of wishing for a change, or preparation for something different in his/her experience. The last 2½ degrees in particular seem to be a wavering time, one of great indecisiveness as the individual experiences an awareness that one's activities in the past are either completed or no longer stimulating to one's growth, and at the same time realizing that it is still too early to commence something new, either because one does not know what to go into, or because one needs more time to prepare before entering into the new activity.

We also notice that about the time a progressed planet reaches 15 degrees of any sign, another turning point is frequently experienced by the native. This is the midway point of a sign, and according to the *common method*, the beginning of the Libra influence. Typically Libra's nature is one again of wavering, but not because of an end or beginning that seems eminent. Rather it is because one is cognizant of the need to create balance in the life, especially in regards to the influence which other people now bring — or create — in the life. One must now make a choice as to which direction to take this activity (it is not a choice as to whether to do it or not, but rather what to do at this time within the activity). At first, there is likely to be the indecision that is so characteristic of Libra, for

6

the individual wants to first of all explore all of the possibilities. Within each possibility lies the pros and the cons, and frequently there is no perfect choice. Eventually the native makes what seems to be the best choice, not only for oneself, but for all who are concerned, because such a choice creates the greatest harmony and balance (either within the self, or around oneself).

Thus the *common method* has observable justification with reference to prognosticative methods like progressions (and probably solar arc directions of the planets as well).

THE TRADITIONAL METHOD

This method is the one used most frequently in the determination of a dwadashamsa. The first 2½ degrees of any sign are assumed to be sub-ruled by the sign itself; the second 2½ degrees by the sign which follows, and so on. For instance, the first 2½ degrees of Virgo is sub-ruled by Virgo (dwad); 2½°-5° Virgo is sub-ruled by the dwad Libra, and so on until 27½°-30° Virgo is seen to be sub-ruled by the Leo dwad.

The idea which supports this system of dwadashamsa determination is akin to that in creating a solar chart when the time of birth is unknown. In the later method, we start the chart with the Sun right on the Ascendant — the beginning of the chart — and assume that the Sun like the Ascendant correlates to the concept of "beginning". Therefore, in this method, the earliest dwadashamsa (the first 2½ degrees) of a sign is assumed to be the point of "beginning" the sign's influence. Furthermore, it is assumed that the beginning of an influence (hence sign) represents its strongest expression — sort of like an <u>explosion</u> of that expression into reality. It is a comparative factor that makes this seem so: because the earlier conditions (i.e. degrees of a former sign) seemed to act a certain way (i.e. have certain characteristics), and the new conditions (i.e. first degrees of the new sign) seem so vastly different, then it appears the earlier part of the experience creates, and thus shapes, the entirety of that which is to follow. Therefore the earlier degrees of the zodiac sign set up the basic characteristics from which the remainder of the sign (i.e. successive degrees) derive their basic tone, essence, or primary characteristics.

In practice we do observe that the earliest degrees of a sign appear greatly different in their expression from the later degrees of the preceding sign. Of course, they are actually different signs, so we would expect this to be the case. At the same time, we might also notice that there is much similarity between early and later degrees of the same sign — much more so than early degrees of one sign and later degrees of the preceding sign, even though the latter are closer together. For instance, Mars in early Aries and late Aries have much in common, though they might be 25 degrees apart, whereas Mars in late Pisces will not have so much in common with an early Aries position of Mars, even though they might be only 5 degrees apart. The change of signs corresponds to a very marked difference in the planet's potential expression. Thus we see that right at the beginning of a sign, the characteristics ascribed to that sign are in effect. And the effect seems very great because of the comparison factor in regards to the sign which precedes it. Therein lies the logical basis for assuming that the first degrees of any sign might be sub-ruled (as a dwad) by that sign itself, and that the following degrees represent modifications to the first degrees.

THE EVOLUTIONARY METHOD

Besides the division of each sign by the number 12, there are other divisions used in the interpretion of different segments of the same sign. For example, it can also be determined that within each dwad, a 12 fold-division can be made to show that each sign is present as a modifying influence within each 2½ degree area.

Since every degree of meridian arc (i.e. Midheaven and Nadir axis) rotates at the approximate rate of one degree per four minutes of time then it can be seen that it takes about ten minutes for the meridian to rotate the distance of a dwadashamsa. It could be assumed that 1/12 of this time — approximately 50 seconds — represents an even finer modification of that dwad — like a sub-dwadashamsa. And within each dwad could potentially appear a sub-dwad of every other sign of the zodiac. This extremely fine division of time — and the zodiac — might have appeal for those individuals who believe that indeed every moment of time has its own unique quality. The more exact the moment being studied is, the more subtle and finer the distinctions and nature of the influences modifying that moment become.

A more common subdivision of signs is that of decanates. This involves a three-fold division of each sign

9

into ten degree segments each. Each decanate of a sign is usually ruled by a sign which is the same element as the major sign itself. For instance, each decanate, or ten-degree division, of Cancer would be a water sign — either Scorpio, Pisces, or Cancer itself.

The decanate system of sign division is used frequently in association with dwadashamsa systems. In the *traditional method* of dwad determination just discussed, the first dwad of each decanate is the same as the decanate itself. For example, the first ten degrees of Scorpio is considered the Scorpio decanate in the *traditional method*. The first 2½ degrees of Scorpio is also considered the Scorpio dwad. The second 10 degrees of Scorpio is sub-ruled by the water sign which follows Scorpio in the natural Zodiac order; thus, 10-20 degrees of Scorpio belongs to the Pisces decanate. The first 2½ degrees of this decanate — or, 10°-12½° of Scorpio — correlates also to the Pisces dwad. 20°-30° Scorpio would then relate to the final water sign, or the Cancer decanate, and its first 2½ degree dwad (20°-22½°) would be that of Cancer.

There is a school of thought which relates decanates and dwadashamsas to yet another principle. This is the *evolutionary*, or *age arc, method* outlined in the book I wrote called <u>Evolutionary Astrology: The Journey Of The Soul Through The Horoscope</u>.[4] This method assumes that each sign has its strongest inherent qualities in the middle section of its 30 degrees. Therefore the second decanate, or ten-twenty degrees, of a sign would correspond to the sign itself, instead of the first ten degrees as in the case of the *traditional method*. For example, in the *evolutionary method*, the first ten degrees of Scorpio would be identified as the water sign _preceding_ Scorpio itself: the Cancer decanate. The middle ten degrees would be ascribed to Scorpio as the decanate, and the final ten degrees (20°-30° Scorpio) would be attributed to the water sign following Scorpio, which would be Pisces.

The idea here is to allow for an evolutionary process within each sign. In other words, no sign — no characteristic which a sign represents — arises out of nothing. There is a developmental process which occurs in the expression of each quality — and those qualities themselves become the basis upon which other qualities are learnt and then expressed. The middle section of a sign then becomes associated with the primary qualities for which that sign represents. The beginning segment of the sign consists of the tools, the resources, the experiences, the underlying qualities necessary for the proper (and possibly forceful) expression of what the sign fully and totally represents. The later segement (the third decanate) of any sign would then correspond to those activities to which this refined, primary force now directs itself. In this directing of self outwardly, even more subtle characteristics are necessary, as implied in the nature of the sign corresponding to this third decanate. Yet through this entire sequence, the major essence of what the sign stands for is intact, for it is the strength which is the middle. As such, this middle section attracts a growth process to occur in the earlier stages (first decanate) and even becomes a guiding force as to how it will develop early in its evolution; and it also controls and shapes the nature of those activities which are a result of its basic qualities (last decanate).

The method of determining dwads by the _evolutio-_

11

nary method is similiar to that used in the *traditional method*. The first 2½ degrees of every decanate is the dwad of the same sign. For instance, 0°-2½° of Libra is the Gemini dwad, because the first decanate of Libra is the air sign preceding Libra, which is Gemini. The next 2½ degrees would be the sign which follows, or the Cancer dwad, and so on. 20°-22½° of Libra would be the Aquarius dwad, for it is the first 2½° of the last Libra decanate, which is in fact Aquarius.

There is still another basis for this method of determining dwadashamsas, and this is a result of study relating to age arcs. In this theory, every degree correlates to a year of life, which repeats itself every 30 years, as there are 30 degrees to a sign. Thus, for instance, the first dwad of the second decanate of any sign (i.e. 10-12½ degrees) becomes associated with ages 10-12½ years, or 40-42½ years, or even 70-72½ years. Based upon the assumptions of the *evolutionary method* and the age arc system, it is not until ages 10-12½ that an individual will manifest fully the expression of a particular sign. Though there will be characteristics expressed earlier which suggest some of the later traits, it is generally agreed upon by students of human behavior that the personality is not that strongly formed in the very early (i.e. at least first seven years) stages of life. In fact, it seems to become most firmly formed during the years 10-20.

The first ten years of a child's life are spent learning within the framework of a family setting. At the very outset, the child is in fact completely dependent upon the parents (or parental figures) for support. So the foundation of the individual's life is cemented with the influences of others who provide, care for, and support the soul. Only during the later part of this phase (i.e.

12

ages 7½-10) does a modification to this basic core begin to take place as the child expands into a social world of peer influences. The child still cannot leave its foundation totally, but preparation for such now gets underway as relationships of value become established outside of the family.

Around the age of ten a child begins to contemplate (though by no means decide) what objective their life might serve, and the consequences of such a direction. In other words, the individual begins to be goal-oriented. Matters like career and vocation, heaven and hell, success and failure start to enter one's consciousness. These thoughts then become the building blocks upon which the core of the adult personality will be formed. Typically this is the stage (age 10-12½) when the individual becomes aware of his/her work (in school or play) in reference, or comparison, to others. The quality, or quantity of work produced determines the judgements of others (like teachers, parents and other authoritarian models) upon him/her, and consequently becomes the source of the most powerful shaping and conditioning processes that will eventually mold this into an adult personality. Of course the judgements never stop — they continue through the remainder of life. But here it is most critical, for here is where sensitivity to judgment commences.

How the individual copes with this phase of life depends a great deal on the nature of the development which took place prior to this time, symbolized by the first decanate of a sign. The manner of coping also determines what that individual will do with the rest of his/her life which follows (third decanate).

If we assume that 10-12½ degrees corresponds, as a

13

dwad, to the sign itself, and that indeed 10-12½ years of life is when the individual starts manifesting the characteristics inherent in that sign, then 7½ years before and after would correspond to those signs which would square the sign itself. The idea of a square is to produce a crisis which, if dealt with properly, results in a character building of the individual. 2½°-5° of any sign would be a dwad which squares the sign; this would also be true of the dwad ruling 17½°-20° of a sign. For instance, 2½°-5° of Capricorn would correspond to the Libra dwad, and 17½-20°, the Aries dwad — both squaring Capricorn. Relating this to age arc, one can readily see that ages 2½-5 years, and 17½-20 years are indeed critical stages in anyone's growth. The earlier age occurs right after the muscular structure and vocal chords have developed, and the child is now expected to communicate ideas, needs and feelings to others without a real command of language (very frustrating). At the same time the child is expected to assume more responsibility for his or her safety when the world is still relatively unfamiliar — and if he/she makes a mistake, the consequence is liable to be some sort of punishment which the child might never understand (i.e. might mistake punishment as a sign of losing the love of a parent, which in turn might be misinterpreted to mean one is unworthy of receiving love from others). It is a potentially frightening period, a time of feeling like "a stranger and afraid in a world I never made."

The later period, 17½-20 years of age, is even more obvious as a critical period of growth. In the American Society — and most Western societies — this is the time of graduation from high school. The decision is:

14

"What do I do and where do I go with my life?" It is usually a time of leaving home, or breaking away from the past. It is also a time when the individual contemplates the merging of the identity with that of another, as in marriage, love, or whatever. A large number of people go through this stage of needing another, and the fear is: "What if they don't want me?" A fear of rejection could lead to inhibition of initiative, or the development of jealousy and prejudice in order to safeguard one's possessions (or ego integrity, which is easily threatened with pain now).

These are just two examples of how age arcs work in a psychological, evolutionary process. Each degree in each sign can be seen to correlate with an age of development which relates to the dwads' aspect formation with the sign itself.

The proof of the validity of age arcs may be observed in the study of planetary degrees. A planet in a particular degree (regardless of sign) will be seen to correlate with a life experience at the same age, and the experience will be of the nature of the planet. For instance, a Venus experience will unfold at the age corresponding to Venus' degree in the chart. It may be a love experience, or the birth of a child who will have Venus qualities, or some other experience which relates to the house, or houses, in which Venus is posited or rules. The same thing applies to other planets. If Mars is in 14 degrees of Taurus, then at age 14 there will be a Martian experience, such as an accident, a separation in love, or possibly a competitive event or a new beginning in the life.

Observing these correlations to be true between planetary degrees and ages of like life experiences, it may be deduced that the degrees do indeed correlate with years of life. This then is the basis for the *evolutionary method* of determining dwadashamsas.

THE CHALDEAN METHOD

Another system of dwadashamsa determination is that which appears in this book. John Sandbach refers to this as the system originated by the ancient Chaldean teachers of astrology, because it is founded upon the principles of the original seven planets.

In *Chaldean method*, the first dwadashamsa assignment is according to the sign co-ruled by the planet having rulership over the sign in question (except with Cancer and Leo). The original seven planets are used (not including Uranus, Neptune and Pluto). Cancer (ruled by the Moon) and Leo (ruled by the Sun) are interchanged with one another. For example, the first 2½ degrees of Sagittarius would be ruled by the other sign which Jupiter co-rules — or, Pisces. The successive dwadashamsas are then assigned according to the natural order of the zodiac (as in all other systems of dwadashamsa determination), so that 2½°-5° of Sagittarius would belong to the Aries dwad, 5°-7½° to Taurus, and so on. In the case of Leo, the first dwad would be sub-ruled by Cancer, and vice-versa.

Sandbach's system is a great deal more elaborate than that of the ancients however. In this book, <u>Dwadashamsas: Degree Analyses And Their Deeper Meanings</u>, he treats us to a fascinating relationship of the dwadashamsas to the major arcana of the Tarot and Numerology. Every symbol in the major arcana is associated with a number, and every number to a zodiac sign or planet. The meaning of every dwadashamsa is then implied in not only the signs involved, but also in the Tarot and numbers which they correspond to. The results are profoundly insightful.

The assumption that the first 2½ degrees of a sign should have characteristics of "the other sign" co-ruled by the same planet, is a thought-provoking idea. It seems to incorporate concepts present in the last two systems. That is, having the first dwad of a sign ruled by the ruling planet of the sign is somewhat similiar to the *tranditional method* — at least from a <u>planetary</u> rulership point of view, though not from a <u>sign</u> point of view. Having a different sign rulership for the first dwad, but nonetheless one which has a relationship to the sign itself (by factor of possessing the same ruling planet) makes this method somewhat akin to the *evolutionary method*. This latter correspondence might suggest that the primary characteristics of a sign (which one would expect to show in the dwad which is the same sign as the entire sign itself) grow out of material, or experience, which precedes that primary segment of the sign. Thus the strongest part of a sign is not the first dwad, but a section which follows — and perhaps is part of a developmental sequence which begins with the first dwad. This is also the basic idea behind the *evolutionary method* of dwadashamsa determination. Yet the first dwad is extremely impor-tant and does possess a definite relationship to the entire sign itself, being that both are ruled by the same planet, and not just being of the same element. The planetary correlation between the entire sign and the first dwad might suggest the "explosion effect" in

17

operation (the observable and significant difference between the last degrees of one sign and the first degrees of the next sign), which we mentioned previously as a basis for assuming validity in the *traditional method*. It thus appears that a logical explanation (though this does not mean it is the correct explanation) for the *Chaldean method* determination of dwadashamsa identification lies in the understanding of a both a developmental, or evolutionary, sequence within the sign itself, and also an "explosion effect", both of which begin with the first dwadashamsa of any sign.

USES OF THE CHALDEAN METHOD

Regardless of the reasons as to why a system might logically work, the true test is whether or not in practice it actually does work.

The most meaningful function of this book will be in a psychological understanding of the factors present at the time of the event to which any horoscope applies. This will usually be the natal chart, though it could also be used just as effectively in an electional or horary chart. Let us assume we wish to test the accuracy of Sandbach's ideas: how would we go about it? We might look up the degree of an individual's natal Sun, or Ascendant, or some other important part of the natal horoscope, and see if the description "fits", or perhaps gives further light in understanding the subject we are examining.

As a test, I decided to do this, using the example of President Jimmy Carter. I chose this first example because I knew the text of this material was written in 1974, long before Sandbach and most of the American

18

public had any knowledge of Mr. Carter's birthdate (let alone existence!). President Carter's natal Sun is about 8° Libra, putting it in the fourth dwad of Libra. Sandbach identifies this as the Leo dwad, and describes it (in part) as follows:

> "This segment is a powerful diplomat . . . relies on its personality to carry it through situations, and attains to positions of power quite easily because it can make itself well-liked with little effort. It has all the outer trappings of a leader, but needs to make this appearance an inner reality as well."

He goes on to describe many other characteristics which I have come to associate with Jimmy Carter's personality.

Another example is the commonly accepted 13° Taurus Ascendant of former President Gerald Ford. Sandbach identifies this as the Pisces dwad of Taurus, and says:

> "This segment is a champion of causes. It attempts to maintain the basic doctrines of whatever movement it associates with."

Further on — almost eerily predictive — Sandbach states:

> "Disappointments which come through friends are often used beneficially to deepen its understanding of human nature. It does not give up easily in friendships . . . (It possesses) staunch devotion (and) does not like to see anything come to an end. When it believes in an idea, its acceptance of it is immovable. It may overjustify itself in an attempt to feel that what it is doing is right."

The use of this book serves equally well when studying the horoscopes of countries. For example, the dis-

19

positor of the Moon in the United States of America's chart is Uranus, which is posited in almost 9° of Gemini. This is the Sagittarius dwad, which also subrules the commonly-believed Gemini Ascendant. Pertaining to this dwad, Sandbach writes:

"This segment is concerned with methods to dominate natural forces. It sees the mind as ruler of the body..."

(i.e. perhaps the emphasis of mental, educational development the U.S.A. seems to concerned with?).

"It bases its judgement of actions (according) to whether or not the actions are effective, rather than if they are good or evil ... This segment feels much more secure when it is well-educated and may manifest a fear of people who know more than it does."

As a reference in understanding parts of a person's — or nation's or event's — personality, this book is invaluable. It has been so "right on" in so many cases I have analyzed. As might be expected, this diagnostic accuracy has further advantages in the fact that such insight serves to facilitate self-understanding and consequent self-unfoldment, which is one of the basic and positive uses of astrology.

In addition to deeper understandings of a particular personality (or facet of a particular part of one's nature), there are several other uses of this book. For one, it may be used effectively in some of the finer points of rectification of a birth time. If the time of birth is unknown, one might examine the various dwads covered in one day by the transiting Moon (it will usually cover 12-15 degrees in a day, or about 5 dwads). By determining which Moon dwad seems most appropriate, one can assume the natal position of the Moon to be in the center of this 2½ degree segment, and if correct, then the time would be within 2½ hours of this time determined (i.e. the Moon's motion is about one degree per two hours of time. In five hours, the Moon would transit approximately 2½ degrees of arc — the space of a dwad. One-half of this distance — the mid-point — would thus correspond to 2½ hours either side).

Even finer details of birth time may be determined when using the Ascendant — or Midheaven — as the point of reference. The Midheaven moves at the rate of almost one degree for every four minutes of time. The Ascendant averages this same rate, though its movement is not consistent as is the Midheaven — sometimes it moves quite a bit more, sometimes a little less, though its average motion over a 24 hour day is one degree per four minutes of time. Therefore a dwad will change on the Meridian approximately every ten minutes, and though more erratic, frequently the same rate applies to the Horizon (i.e. Ascendant-Descendant). Therefore in the final steps of rectification, an analysis of the different dwads for the angles — especially the Midheaven and Ascendant — could become a helpful and determining factor in choosing the correct time.

Using President Carter's horoscope again, this method can be seen to be useful. Most reliable sources indicate that Jimmy Carter was born October 1, 1924, at 7:00 AM near Archery, Georgia. A slight controversy exists as to whether or not this is Eastern, or Central Standard Time. The former yields an 11 degree Libra Ascendant, while a CST of birth would give

Mr. Carter a 26 degree Libra rising. A majority of astrologers use the 26 degree Libra Ascendant, assuming the time was based upon Central Standard clock time. Let us see what Sandbach says of these different dwads:

11° Libra (Virgo dwad): "(This segment) wants to base its actions on precise methods. This segment wants to do the most effective thing it can do at every moment of its existence. Therefore it is a planner. It wants to solve its problems with a minimum of wasted effort . . . This segment desires smooth, harmonious, and coordinated activity more than anything. It is busy all the time. . . . It senses that its existence is for some definite purpose . . . Therefore it cannot become involved in anything in which it does not have intimately personal feelings for. Conversely it always brings a uniqueness of self into all of its endeavors."

26° Libra (Pisces dwad): "It is necessary for this segment to live by routines, to make its activities consistent, logical and ordered so that it can experience a steady progression of accomplishment. It has a strong desire to give to other people — to work for their happiness. It goes out of its way to be self-sacrificing, and can be very devoted to a cause. . . . There can be a lot of selfishness here becuase of an inflexible nature. It feels it has to serve in its own way and will give of itself only on its own terms. It may not want to try to change itself or to understand someone else's viewpoint. Its attraction to others can be obsessive . . . it must be true to itself not as a matter of morality, but because it can be no other way. It may be unable to do (things) alone and for itself those things which it could do for someone else it wants to please, and it is this impulse of loving subjugation to others which triggers its productivity . . . the breaking off of close bonds of love could be

22

devastating, and it will go out of its way to prevent this."

Due to the nature of similarities between Pisces and Virgo (the two dwads involved here), there are many like qualities involving service. However, the Virgo dwad describes quite accurately the activity which the public notices about President Carter: his need to do things effectively, smoothly, harmoniously, and his dislike for wasted efforts. He certainly seems very busy all the time, and in many instances he has related his sense of having a definite — even devine — purpose in the affairs of this world.

The later dwad speaks heavily of a life of service and self-sacrifice, and of a manner which finds it difficult to understand the viewpoints of others. I for one do not believe Mr. Carter is so driven to do things with the characteristic of self-sacrifice, nor does he seem closed-minded to ideas which are different than his own, finding it most difficult to bend. To the contrary, one of the greatest criticisms directed towards him has been his tendency to agree with the ideas of too many conflicting and different view points! Newspapers have oftentimes editorialized about Mr. Carter's fence-sitting, whereby he supports one group one day, and the next day claims to support a group which stands for the apparently opposite principles. It furthermore does not seem that he is unable to do things independently of others, for many of his decisions to date have been not been according to the desires of his closest political advisers, nor according to the majority of the American public (i.e. amnesty-granting and the Panama Canal Treaty).

If John Sandbach's description of each of these

dwads is accurate, then it seems to me that the 11° Libra Ascendant is more fitting of Mr. Carter's behavior and style. This of course would mean that the 7:00 AM Eastern Standard Time is correct (or close), and not Central Standard Time.

The uses of these descriptions of dwadashamsas is practically unlimited. They may be used to gain deeper insights into the meaning of one's dreams, by drawing up a horary chart upon awakening and analyzing the different degree areas which stand out. They may be used in understanding the changes within one's life, by analyzing the various degrees areas highlighted in the progressions, or solar arc directions in one's horoscope. As already seen, they may be used in the art of rectification, and also in the further understanding of countries, businesses, or any thing to which an electional horoscope might apply.

But the primary use of these dwads, in my estimation, will be in the understanding of human behavior — in the analysis of motivations, styles, and personal characteristics which make a person what he/she is. I suggest the reader pay especial attention to the dwads which contain the Sun and the Ascendant, since in my study these seem to yield the most insightful results. But also look at the other important parts of a chart — the Moon, the Nadir and Midheaven, the Descendant, the ruler of the horoscope and the depositor of the Sun, the culminating and rising planets, and even the angular midpoints. For me this book is a joy; it is a joy because it is extremely fascinating and revealing, and because I believe it is the most insightful book of its kind now available.

I hope you, the reader, find this book as valuable in your study and practice of astrology as I have. Thank you, John, for writing such a masterpiece.

Ray Merriman
April 24, 1978

BIBLIOGRAPHY AND SUGGESTED READING

1. Raman, B.V., Hindu Predictive Astrology, India Book House 1972
2. Carter, Charles, An Encyclopedia of Psychological Astrology, Theosophical Publishing House, London 1963
3. Wemyss, Maurice, The Wheel Of Life or Scientific Astrology, L.N. Fowler & Co., London (no date given)
4. Merriman, Raymond A., Evolutionary Astrology: The Journey Of The Soul Through The Horoscope, Seek-It Publications, Rochester, Michigan 1977

   De Luce, Robert, Constellational Astrology, De Luce Publishing Co., Los Angeles, California 1963

   Sakoian, Francis & Aker, Louis, The Zodiac Within Each Sign, Francis Sakoian, 1977

25

1 CHAPTER ONE
SUB-RULERSHIPS
OF DWADASHAMSAS

The dwadashamsas are 2½° divisions of the zodiac.

There are 144 dwadashamsas in the entire zodiac, twelve in each sign.

Just as a sign is a complete function within itself — a mirror of the whole zodiac — a dwadashamsa reflects the sign's relationship to the whole. Therefore this system of division is a study of completeness. Each dwadashamsa (or dwad, for short) reflects a potential perfection of functioning within a complete cycle.

It has only been since the recent publication (1972) of Carl Payne Tobey's <u>Astrology Of Inner Space</u> that the sub-rulerships of these dwads have been made widely known. It was earlier thought that they followed a cycle starting with Aries; that is, the first dwadashamsa of each sign was believed to be sub-ruled by Aries, the second dwad by Taurus, and so on through the natural succession of signs.

Another school of thought believed the first dwadashamsa of a sign was ruled by the sign itself; that is, for example, the first dwad of Virgo is ruled by Virgo, the next by Libra, and so on.

The system of sub-rulerships set forth in this book is based upon the planets, or more precisely, that which is known as the Chaldean order of planets. That system involves only those planets which the eye may see (i.e. all those contained within the orbit of Saturn). These five visible planets, plus the Sun and our Earth's own Moon, are seven in number and allude to a natural pairing of the zodiac signs. The Sun and

Moon, called the "lights", pair the signs Leo and Cancer respectively. The other five planets account for two signs each, in a very well defined order. According to proximity to the Sun, each planet rules in order both the signs which *follow* Leo, and *precede* Cancer, as follows:

Cancer	— Moon/Sun	— Leo
Gemini	— Mercury	— Virgo
Taurus	— Venus	— Libra
Aries	— Mars	— Scorpio
Pisces	— Jupiter	— Sagittarius
Aquarius	— Saturn	— Capricorn

The first dwadashamsa of any sign is sub-ruled by the sign which is a planetary companion to itself. Thus the first dwad of Aries is sub-ruled by Scorpio, since Scorpio is the "other" sign ruled by Mars, which rules Aries. The next dwad of Aries is sub-ruled by Sagittarius, the next by Capricorn, and so on according to the natural order of the zodiac.

These interpretations of the dwadashamsas have been written with the help of the Egyptian Tarot of C. C. Zain. In this Tarot, every sign and planet is assigned a numerical value. These values may be added and subtracted to yield yet other numbers which are keys to the meaning of combinations. The Tarot is the Great Book of Thoth, with movable pages whose vast possibilities of rearrangement contain all the archetypal truths of the universe.

Any final sum which is over 22, such as the case when Gemini (the Star, card #17) combines with Leo (the Sun, card #19) to yield 36, is reduced by adding its digits. In the example just presented, 36 would become 3 + 6, or 9. Nine is the number of Aquarius, meaning that the combination of hope and faith, or truth (the meaning of the card for Gemini), with will power and creativity (the meaning of the card for Leo) produces knowledge and wisdom, which is the meaning for the Aquarius card.

There is only one card which will appear as the sum of two others in every sign. This is card #21, called the Adept, and ruled by the Sun. It always in the 5°-7½° segment of each sign. This implies the position of the Sun as the supreme ruler in the cosmic scheme.

Mr. Tobey's suggestion of a clockwise house system, which begins with Virgo ruling the twelfth house, has also been contemplated. This system puts the third house (counting backwards from the twelfth) at what is usually referred to as the tenth house — the Midheaven house. From this point of view, it seems quite significant that the third dwadashamsa of every sign numerically adds up to #21, ruled by the Sun. This implies that the will (Sun) is ideally directed through the conscious mind (tenth house, Midheaven), which is the highest position in the sky. Also, if Virgo rules the twelfth house, and Libra the eleventh, then Scorpio rules the tenth. Scorpio is the card of the Sovereign, and represents realization. Hence each sign is ideally capable of realization (Scorpio) through conscious direction (tenth house) of the will (Sun).

There is much more to be understood about these dwadashamsas. It is the author's hope to one day write a book dealing with the esoteric implication of dwadashamsa in relationship to house systems and spiritual regeneration.

2 CHAPTER TWO
ASTRO-NUMEROLOGY

Astrology derives from two sources: outside, factual information, and the Self. Outside information is the input, and the Self is the refiner of ideas. Therefore there are two processes occuring simultaneously: one *quantitative* and undifferentiated (outside information, sensory impressions, etc.) or empirical, and the other *qualitative*, formal and catagorical (the Self).

Astro-numerology is basically derived from the second (Self) process. Numbers are a structure basic to all reality, and as our thinking process encounters this structure, we learn via a process of refinement from ourselves.

The greatest potential danger with numerology is that it is so abstract. A person is liable to project any idea on any set of numbers. Numbers are complete. There is even a number for nothing (zero). Numbers project from nothing to infinity, yet they have a definite form and structure.

In the system of astro-numerology used in this book, there are ten root numbers spanning from zero to nine, with zero counted as a term. All numbers have their symbolism derived from these nine root numbers plus zero. Zero however projects and generates nothing but itself.

Zero is the blank stage upon which the play of numbers present themselves to consciousness, much as Tao underlies the play of the relative, of Yin and Yang. The human ideal is to become zero — to become the stage. Astrologically zero is associated with the Earth and Pluto.

Pluto, in astrology, is seen as the individual's will to power, an unnecessary complexity when projected onto the material world, i.e. politics, gangsterism. In its more positive expression, Pluto might denote the power which emanates in a controlled, natural and graceful manner from the self-realized individual. Is one earthbound and becoming more earthbound, or is one projecting his/her ideals out beyond the solar system through the divine obsession symbolized by Pluto, which projects toward a central point of cosmic awareness far beyond our own Sun? Zero is the all or nothing number: zero and infinity.

Pluto adds nothing to another planet-it merely intensifies it. It adds nothing to a sign-it merely lends the sign so much power that its potential becomes nothing less than angelic or demonic. As one proceeds to finer and finer levels there is more and more power. For instance, there is more power released by an atomic reaction than by a chemical reaction involving the same quantity of material. At the point of nothingness is infinite power. Such is the nature of Pluto, and of the number zero.

The number one is the first tangible number, the progenitor of number. Thus one symbolizes *unity*, and therefore mind, or the Platonic 'ideal' as opposed to relative perfection as in the Greek mind which would not allow for the extremes of nothingness and infinity. One, or unity, is astrologically represented by Mercury (mind). Mind is universal: we are not pieces of reality, we are reality — in fact, the only reality. Mind is the unifying factor of self and reality.

Two is *duality*, and in astrology correlates to Virgo. It is body as opposed to mind. We can say that all is one, but we live in a world of twos, i.e. sexes, day and night, good and evil, you and me, etc. Virgo governs purification and perfection as the purpose of relative reality is to perfect the self. Virgo is the illusion that opposing forces exist. At root, it is the dichotomy between something (one) and nothing (zero). When the mind becomes aware of its matrix — nothingness — then it becomes dual (two minds, or Virgo). The potential for analysis is then born, and analysis is a key word of Virgo. Virgo also rules health, and Man's greatest dichotomy is the mind-body. Mercury is exalted in Virgo because it is the mind which potentially can harmonize, and thus control, the body.

Three is associated with Libra. Mind (one) plus duality (two) yields *activity* and the results of activity. Libra is a dynamic relationship which produces movement. Mind always seeks to balance (Libra) when it encounters relative reality. Virgo is a mutable sign because of the changeable nature of duality. Libra is a cardinal sign because the process of attaining balance is an assertive and self-initiatory process.

Four is represented by the sign of Scorpio. Mind (one) combines with activity and productivity (three) to achieve *realization* (four). Realization cannot be taken away, as implied by the fact that Scorpio is a fixed sign.

Thus far one-half of the numbers have been discussed: zero, one, two, three, and four. This is actually five terms, and in the Tarot, the number five represents Man who is the *harmonizer* and coordinator of these five factors. The number five corresponds to Jupiter, which rules religion — a necessary invention of Man, and a tool for his self-perfection.

31

Now harmony can be built on either a temporary or eternal basis. One has a choice, and the mind (one) makes the choice as to how it is going to harmonize (five) itself. This choice, then, becomes symbolized by the number six — Venus. Venus rules one's *values*, which at any time, one believes will bring harmony. If one chooses a superficial or incomplete set of values, and establishes a momentary harmony, then eventually the end result will be discord. Most astrologers are aware of the disruptive and upsetting potential of Venus when improperly expressed.

Human life is designed for success. If one does not succeed, then he/she will have to try again. Human beings cannot do otherwise. So mind (one) eventually chooses the correct path, the correct set of values (six) and is *victorious* (seven). Seven corresponds to Sagittarius, or mind over matter, the Spirit dominating material reality. Matter is also Spirit, as both are energy, but the energy of Spirit is subtle, while that of matter is dense. The finer always dominates the denser levels.

When the mind attempts domination (one plus seven), it creates *karma* — the law of cause and effect — which is associated with Capricorn (eight). Eight is also crystallization since it is a balancing of realization (four plus four — realization against realization). This can lead to stagnation or to justice. Therefore Capricorn also rules justice.

When the mind (one) becomes aware of its karma (eight) *wisdom* (Aquarius) is generated. Wisdom is also victory (seven) over relativity (two), balancing (three) of values (six), and realization (four) of harmony (five).

32

As previously stated, all other numbers and their meanings are derived from these nine (ten, counting zero). These first ten terms are on the level of *unity*, the level of awareness of the absolute, represented by Mercury. The next nine numbers, 10-18, are on the second level, and hence the Virgo (two) level. The second level numbers (10-18) mirror the first nine numbers through a sort of relativity. For instance, mind (one) on the relative level (nine plus one) becomes *individuality* as it now loses its universality. In astrology, individuality comes under the rule of Uranus. Mind appears eccentric on the level of duality, hence the association of Uranus with eccentricity. Duality overshadows the mind here. However, when the mind shines through duality, there is intuition, which is also a characteristic of Uranus.

The number eleven is two on the level of two (two plus nine). Eleven is the number of force and/or power. In astrology, this relates to Neptune. Dualism on its own level generates tension or force. Neptune rules the double-bodied sign of Pisces. Pisces governs belief, and anything that is believed 'out-pictures' everything else contrary to it, and if believed long enough and strongly enough will become a reality. Hence *power* (eleven) and mind (one) combine to produce *belief* (twelve), ruled by Pisces.

Aries is number 13. Thirteen is four on the second level (four plus nine), or realization on the level of relativity. This produces *change* and *transformation*, which is the function of Aries.

All other numbers on the second level have their meanings derived in a similiar manner. Thus:

14 is harmonization (5) on the relative level (9),

producing *regeneration* in the material realm (Taurus).

15 is values (6) on the relative plane (9) yielding material *structure* (Saturn) of physical reality.

16 is victory (7) on the relative plane (9), which creates physical *initiative* (Mars).

17 is balance (8) on the relative plane (9). The result of such balance and justice is *perception* which crystalizes (or gives meaning to) relativity (Gemini).

18 is wisdom (9) on the second level (9) of relativity. Relative wisdom pertains to the areas of *emotion* and *feelings* (Cancer).

There are yet four more numbers on a third level: 19, 20, 21, and 22. The third level corresponds to the plane of the number three — activity and fruitfulness. 19 is one on the level of three (1+9+9). Hence it represents the *mind in activity* (Leo).

20 is duality (2) on the plane of activity (9+9), or *dual activity* (Moon).

21 is three on the level of three, or fruitfulness on the level of activity. Hence it is *fruitful activity* (Sun).

22 is realization (four) in the realm of activity (third level), or realization of one's work to do (i.e. *realization of destiny*). This is governed by Pluto, which also rules the term zero.

This is a mere capsulization of the principles used in this book. The reader may use this numerological pattern to study anything in astrology. For instance, consider the combination of Venus in Cancer: Venus is six and Cancer is 18 (6+18=24). 24 is 6 on the third plane (6+9+9). Hence values (six) on the plane of activity (3rd level) produces an active appreciation of things (Venus = appreciation). This could potentially

34

express itself in an active interest or involvement in the arts, or a giving (fruitful — third level) love nature (Venus).

This numerological pattern is a mandala — a structured system that can be contemplated upon for an unlimited source of information. As it is explored and used, this system of stimulating thought will become clearer and clearer in one's mind.

In addition, this system has a direct relationship to the houses of the horoscope, which operates in the manner presented in example and table 1.

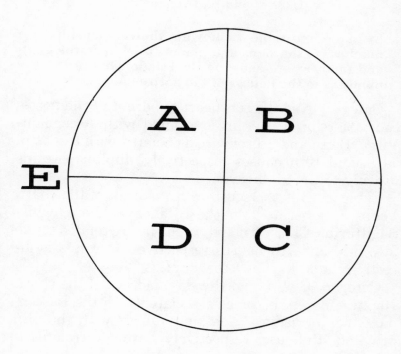

TABLE 1

Category A
1 = Mercury (planet)
2 = Virgo (sign)
3 = Libra (sign)
4 = Scorpio (sign)
5 = Jupiter (planet)

Category B
6 = Venus (planet)
7 = Sagittarius (sign)
8 = Capricorn (sign)
9 = Aquarius (sign)
10 = Uranus (planet)

Category C
11 = Neptune (planet)
12 = Pisces (sign)
13 = Aries (sign)
14 = Taurus (sign)
15 = Saturn (planet)

Category D
16 = Mars (planet)
17 = Gemini (sign)
18 = Cancer (sign)
19 = Leo (sign)
20 = Moon (planet)

Category E
21 = Sun (planet)
22 = Pluto/Earth (planet)

Example and table 1: showing the relationship of numbers to the signs and planets used in astrology, and furthermore showing the relationship of these numbers to the houses of the horoscope.

Category A is the southeast quadrant of the horoscope. Mercury is herein associated with Ascendant. Virgo, Libra and Scorpio are associated with the 12th, 11th, and 10th houses respectively. Jupiter pertains directly to the Midheaven.

Category B is the southwest quadrant of the chart. Venus is associated to the Midheaven here, while Sagittarius, Capricorn and Aquarius are related to the 9th, 8th, and 7th houses respectively. Uranus is directly related to the Descendant.

Category C is the northwest quadrant of the chart. Neptune herein becomes associated with the Descendant, while Pisces, Aries, and Taurus with the 6th, 5th, and 4th houses respectively. Saturn correlates to the Nadir point.

Category D is the northeast section of the horoscope. Mars is associated with the Nadir in this segment, while Gemini, Cancer and Leo relate to the 3rd, 2nd, and 1st houses respectively. The Moon directly applies to the Ascendant in this quadrant.

Category E applies entirely to the Ascendant.

This system of house rulerships is strictly esoteric. It is an ideal inner arrangement as opposed to the usual outer, and "real" arrangement used in more mundane astrology. Actually it is this arrangement that might correctly be considered the "real" one, since the outer reality is itself a dualistic — and hence illusionary — reality.

The following is a basic interpretation of the signs and planets corresponding to the houses and angles in this system:

Category A:

Ascendant/Mercury (1): Mind is always moving and in a state of becoming. Thus it is associated with the eastern angle (Ascendant), or the direction which the Earth turns, thereby allowing things to become visible.

12th house/Virgo (2): That which is hidden and in need of analysis and purification. The twelfth house is the house of dawning, as the Sun is here at dawn. This symbolizes the dawning of the mind into relativity, or, reincarnation.

11th house/Libra (3): The hopes and wishes which are the focal point for the self's activity and bringing of things to fruition.

10th house/Scorpio (4): In one sense, the social position and career. More basic though, it is the house where realization is achieved. An individual's karma is bound up with others, and one's realization thus depends upon others. One must affirm and support the positive dictates of society (and deny that which is negative).

Midheaven/Jupiter (5): The goal of life, or expansive harmonization.

Category B:

Midheaven/Venus (6): The goal of life inextricably bound up in choice and values.

9th house/Sagittarius (7): All the tools and/or instruments one needs to dominate the mind and achieve spiritual victory. Thus it relates to education, religion and philosophy.

8th house/Capricorn (8): Transmutation which is effected through the law of karma, or cause and effect. Death, in this sense, is the greatest balancing factor in one's experience.

7th house/Aquarius (9): The experiences, and instruments, which foster one's growth of wisdom, as in one to one relationships like marriage and partnerships.

Descendant/Uranus (10): The outside world as opposed to the self which is symbolized by the Ascendant. It is in these outer realms that the creative individuality, the uniqueness symbolized by Uranus in the individual, should manifest.

Category C:

Descendant/Neptune (11): The point where power should be used. Obligation is a key word for Neptune, and power brings with it great responsibility. One has an obligation to use power correctly, for the right reasons, and for the betterment of all those he/she contacts.

6th house/Pisces (12): The dedication one has for work, service, and even health. The Pisces card in the Tarot is called the martyr, and in a sense, ill health is akin to being martyred to one's own negativity.

5th house/Aries (13): Creative self-expression which is ever-changing and transforming the self in its activity.

4th house/Taurus (14): Harmonization and regeneration within the inner self, to establish the sense of the Soul's home. Outwardly, the physical home.

Nadir/Saturn (15): That structure which underlies everything. The Nadir is the point furthest below (under) the Earth. Structure implies fate, and in this context, both the structure and the fate are hidden.

Category D:

Nadir/Mars (16): The source of initiative force which is propelled outwardly from the unseen. The primordial energy within the essence of each living organism.

3rd house/Gemini (17): That perception which allows the individual to relate to duality, truth, hope and faith. The ability to communicate this perception gives one hope, and the ability to see truth.

2nd house/Cancer (18): In the Tarot, Cancer is associated with mediumship. Matter is the medium (or resource — 2nd house) of Spirit. The Medium's *body* is his/her medium for contact with Spirit, and thus the 2nd house is associated with the physical being. One's

body also symbolizes one's primary possession —
another 2nd house keyword.

1st house/Leo (19): The fixed and fiery nature of the
perfected being, who acts out the role of a perfect
avatar before attaining to it.

Ascendant/Moon (20): As the Moon rules cycles, it is
associated with the place where all signs rise.

Category E:

Ascendant/Sun (21): The will, which should always
be in complete alignment with the individuality (sym-

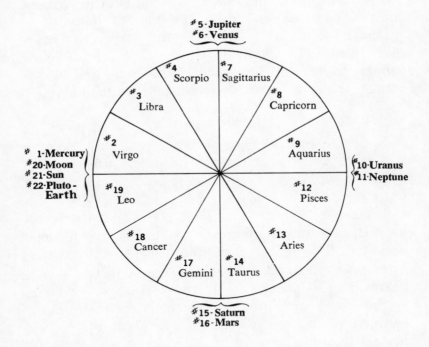

Figure 2

bolized by the cusp of the first house, or Ascendant).

Ascendant/Earth/Pluto (22): The Ascendant is the point of mind (Mercury), the kinetic cycles (Moon), and the potential perfection of individuality (Sun), and is thus associated with the tremendous force of Pluto which operates in the here and now of Earth.

A diagramatic scheme of this system relating numerology and astrological house and angle rulerships is shown in figure 2.

3 CHAPTER THREE
THE DWADASHAMSAS AND THEIR MEANINGS

With an understanding of how the meanings of the dwadashamsas are being derived, it is now possible to proceed to an interpretation of each of these 2½ degree segments of the zodiac. Once again the reader is asked to bear in mind the nature of any planet located in these dwads, as that planet's own nature will have a tremendous coloring effect upon the degrees' natural expression.

In the list of dwadashamsas which follows, the first identification is to the zodiac degrees being discussed. For instance, every paragraph on a new dwad begins with the 2½ zodiac degrees being analyzed, such as 0°-2½° Aries, or 2½°-5° Aries. The second identification is the dwadashamsa correlating to this zodiac degrees segment — itself given in terms of a zodiac sign. To illustrate, the first description begins with: Aries 0°-2½°, *Scorpio*. Scorpio is the dwadashamsa sub-ruling the first 2½ degrees of the sign Aries.

Next a description of the particular dwadashamsa is given, based upon the system of numerology discussed in the last chapter, and also a combination of the characteristics usually applied to both the sign itself and the dwad of the sign. Finally this astrological combination is related to the Tarot as a means of precipitating further insight into the nature of these combinations of sign, number, and dwad.

Aries 0°-2½° *Scorpio:*
The first segment of Aries is sub-ruled by Scorpio (dwadashamsa). Scorpio signifies the individual creat-

ing its own world out of its own personal resources. Aries is the pioneer, symbolizing one who seeks out new realms to conquer. Here the pioneer is most apt to follow its own personal aspirations rather than pooling its energies into group concerns. The leadership qualities of Aries are strongly evident here — the individual wants to be in the forefront of any adventure attempted. It may seek out crisis situations as a means of making sure that it has the ability to take command of them.

This segment does stand for too many routines in life, or for overly predictable living patterns. It has a propensity to constantly re-create a sense of freshness and newness in whatever it is doing.

It does not want to walk in the footsteps of others, but instead desires to blaze its own path. For this reason it oftentimes makes life overly difficult for itself, since it rarely allows itself to be guided, counselled, or told what to do.

Rather than waiting for changes in the life, this individual would prefer to create them when it wants them — even if this causes temporary turmoil.

The Tarot: Aries (The Reaper, #13), combines with Scorpio (The Sovereign, #4) to produce Gemini (The Star, #17). Hence realization has a transforming power which leads to hope and faith in the future. Change implies chance for greater self-knowledge.

Aries 2½°-5° *Sagittarius:*

This segment never gives up, as it possesses a great love for challenge and the meeting of it with much enthusiasm. Its desires may go into a dormant state, but they may be reactivated at any time. This individual tends to excuse any failures as soon as they become a part of the past.

Transformation is a means of re-awakening that eternal quality in which one was, is, and always will be. The Spirit is a denial of death.

This segment always reaches a point in its existence where being self-assertive is vital to its sense of truth. It can conceal its motives only on a temporary basis. Eventually these motives must manifest directly and full-blown. This segment desires to be "everything," because it fears limitation.

Problem-solving is usually attempted by changing the circumstances which surround the individual, rather than attempting an internal change of attitude. Mental attitude is the basis of all functioning and this segment's attitude toward change is so positive that its approach to anything new gives it a sound basis for ultimate success. As long as it can feel a growth process, it is unafraid of any pains or turmoil which may result from the regeneration occurring within.

This segment often experiences vast upheavals in its religious or philosophical beliefs — not in terms of negating existing attitudes, but a deepening and expanding of old concepts.

Often there is a sense of freedom in spending money, especially on travel.

The Tarot: Aries, (The Reaper, #13), combines with Sagittarius, (The Conquerer, #7), to produce the Moon, (The Sarcophagus, #20). Hence, transformation always retains the original essence, and in this manner revitalizes the old and worn out, making it new again.

Aries 5°-7½° *Capricorn:*

This segment expresses conflict with emphasis on immediate involvement. This is the first uncon-ditioned desire to be useful, to hold practical aspira-tion, and to somehow achieve its desires.

Practicality is here, but it is naive and uncon-ditioned. This segment tries to disperse obstacles by menacing threats of force, or by avoiding the obstacle entirely. There may be conflicts between the personal-ity and the career and difficulty in dealing with au-thority, because it wants to try something new, even if the old and established has proven itself of value. It may be destructive in its attempts to improve things. When thrown off balance, it changes its outer course rather than making internal adjustments.

There is great caution here, but the difficulty lies in trying to keep this caution foremost over the innate Aries impulsiveness. A tendency towards outbursts is indicated.

Changes which occur are for the purpose of achiev-ing greater stability. Here the desire for stability is immediate and critical. Its manifestation aids the de-velopment of the will.

This segment learns many simple but useful skills.
The Tarot: Aries, (The Reaper, #13), combines with Capricorn, (The Balance, #8), to produce the Sun, (The Adept, #21). Hence, equilibrium is the key to the transformation which leads to development of the will, the ability to change outwardly yet retain inner consistency.

Aries 7½°-10° *Aquarius:*

This segment desires knowledge, but without loss of

45

innocence. It may lack ability to learn from experience and may make the same mistakes over and over before it recognizes the need to relearn.

Sudden exertion of force and sudden self-realizations are indicated. There is constant searching for new friends. This segment tends to seek out friends who will be supportive, and may achieve through this support.

These people want to feel important, significant and yet worthy.

This segment is far-sighted, broad minded and free thinking. It makes a good friend because of its ability to give kind and friendly criticism. It is quick to correct encountered wrongs. If other things in the chart support it, there may be mechanical ability and inventiveness. This segment signifies "openness to change".

The Tarot: Aries, (The Reaper, #13), combines with Aquarius, (The Sage, #9), to produce Pluto, (The Materialist, #22). Transformation brings the ability to recognize the illusion of the material world, and a desire to look beyond it.

Aries 10°-12½° *Pisces:*

Gullability: beliefs are strong and may stem from ideas that are very ancient or very modern. There is strong self-dependency and faith in the possibility of ultimate self-perfection. This segment tends to be willing to try again, even after severe failure. The very thought of a new beginning will provoke hope of victory. It tends to look beyond what would be called an ultimate and final end. Its belief in itself may be hidden, but is very much there. There is a childlike directness here, and a difficulty in believing that anyone would decieve them.

There is a love of mysterious signs and symbols because they spur the imagination. This segment would be more intrigued by the moods these symbols evoke, than by their actual objective meaning. It is courageous in facing its limitations. It is intrigued by the most current thoughts and concepts, no matter how fallacious they may be, and might even put forth some new concepts of its own. It learns by mimickry.

This segment often displays a complete acceptance of unforseen turns in its destiny. It needs to meet the future with relaxed composure, and not rebell against its lot in life. All this spells "submission to change."

The Tarot: Aries, (The Reaper, #13), combines with Pisces, (The Martyr, #12) to produce Sagittarius (The Conquerer, #7). Hence, transformation is something which is accepted and this passive approach to personal fortune is its means of triumph.

Aries 12½°-15° *Aries:*

This segment manifests new beginnings. It shows great bursts of energy at the starting line, but lack of endurance. It jumps to conclusions.

It is much better at evoking enthusiasm in others than at trying to take on projects single-handedly. The headstrong nature of Aries is in full bloom here. This segment likes to be at the front of any group; more as a scout and trailblazer than as an administrator. There is the true spirit of adventure here. It may be somewhat undiscriminating in the enterprises it undertakes, because its true love is the enterprise itself, not what it encompasses. This segment appreciates any-

47

thing experimental, no matter how shoddy or meaningless it may be. It respects "attempts", regardless of success or failure.

There is a love of bright colors and an identification with children and childhood. It is concerned over its intelligence and desires to improve it. Possible aesthetic skill is indicated.

The Tarot: Aries (The Reaper, #13) combines with Aries (The Reaper, #13) to produce Capricorn (The Balance, #8). Hence, transformation is an end in itself. Its purpose is always an attempt to strengthen weaknesses and reach perfection.

Aries 15°-17½° *Taurus:*

A need to live for the moment. This segment does not like to plan for the future but would rather create the future now. It changes its mind a great deal and appears unpredictable. It can attack challenges with an unrelenting stubbornness.

Its most important aspect is its ability to regenerate and renew through immediate action. It feels inhibited by set patterns and modes of functioning. It craves new experience to rejuvenate itself when it has become worn out or bored with routine. It is concerned with the conservation of its energies, so will never push itself to the point of exhaustion.

Its means of self-expression is usually direct and truthful. It can be quite blunt without meaning to hurt. It will not tolerate anything which oppresses it, and is adept at delivering itself from what ever shackles it.

It makes freedom a way of life, and will react adversely to anyone it feels is trying to possess it, pin it down, or tell it what to do. It needs free air and open space, and will protect its freedom stubbornly. Some may say that it is unable to give of itself.

Like Odysseus, it is striving to find a home, a place of rest, or at least it says so. Actually it quite enjoys its adventures though it could put down roots if the situation were close to ideal.

It usually becomes more conservative as it grows older or at least more adept at making decisions.

The Tarot: Aries, (The Reaper, #13), combines with Taurus, (The Alchemist, #14), to produce Aquarius, (The Sage, #9). Hence, transformation is a means of bringing forces into dynamic equilibrium, which eventually will produce widsom.

Aries 17½°-20° *Gemini:*

This segment can find a way out. It is never at a loss when it comes to escaping from a suffocating situation. As long as it is in the process of going from one thing to another, it feels contented. It likes activity.

It is not interested in passing judgements on things because it is aware that nothing is ever fully completed. It has difficulty isolating one experience from another because of its awareness of the eternal qualities of change. It likes to talk with people, and it is usually easy to know.

It loves to study things independently, and without formal instruction. It draws its own conclusions from what it learns and changes its mind accordingly. It may manifest a lack of discipline and an inability to apply itself consistently in a single direction. It has much nervous energy.

It is a master of suspended judgement. Its initial

49

thoughts are often incisive, but it is loathe to draw logical conclusions from them. Its mind is forceful, but it may rethink something so many times that confusion is the result.

It is not particularly courageous, although others may see it as being so. This stems from a kind of ignorance of danger. Its innocent faith in the law of constant change makes it hopeful even when down, since it knows that things must get better.

The Tarot: Aries, (The Reaper, #13), combines with Gemini, (The Star, #17), to produce Libra, (Isis Unveiled, #3). Hence, transformation and change, when it is backed by hope and faith in guidance from higher planes, will always compel one to act.

Aries 20°-22½° *Cancer:*

A great love of taking chances: This segment is insatiable in its drive to brave the unknown, because it yearns for self-realization. It strives to temper itself like steel. It has the ability to produce surprisingly successful results through the use of dangerous means. It likes to rely on itself and its own judgments rather than to put its fate into another's hands. It has a certain sense of dislocation, in that it can feel any place as its home, without becoming attached to any particular place. It derives security from being "foot-loose."

This segment is intent on learning arts of self-defense, and using them by seeking out dangerous situations.

In terms of creativity, it attempts to push the materials it uses to the very limits of their expressive potential. Its aesthetics are based on dynamic sensuality.

It is highly uncompromising. It will put itself in an insecure position to build up its resistance. It may scorn the idea of self-preservation. It relates romantically to the idea of battling openly with the forces of evil.

It gravitates toward a cataclysmic approach to existence rather than a pattern of natural and steady growth. It would rather try to change something completely and suddenly than by degrees.

It often sees itself as a revealer of mysteries and secrets, because it is unafraid to go where others might fear to tread.

It becomes bored easily and will immediately push on to new territory when it feels there is no more to be discovered.

The Tarot: Aries, (The Reaper, #13), combines with Cancer, (The Moon, #18), to produce Scorpio, (The Sovereign, #4). Hence, transformation which is complete in its effects on all levels of being, brings one to cosmic awareness. To be able to change, even in the face of the unknown, promises growth in consciousness.

Aries 22½°-25° *Leo:*

Much dramatic self-expression: a desire to be creative: this segment is happiest when in the process of doing things. It experiences the creative process as something magical. It feels movement and change as a source of happiness.

It may manifest a self-immolation complex, in that it wants to encompass more and more, so that it can relate to the world on a complete basis. It does not like relationships that fall too much into set patterns. It cannot and will not leave well enough alone, and takes the attitude that "the best is barely good enough."

It is agressive in its attempts to find a broader basis of ecstatic action, and will not try to fall back on its past accomplishments.

Uncertainty, strangely enough, is a source of security, for it sees life as a constant dawning. The best thing it can do, to be both content with itself and successful in its affairs, is to be completely itself, and to take a direct approach in its dealings with others.

It is always ready to take advice and criticism and is easily coached by others. It is naturally generous and will not think twice about spending its energies and resources, for it has a deep faith in the constant renewal of all things. It would rather keep goods in a state of circulation and exchange than to hoard and save for some uncertain future.

The Tarot: Aries (The Reaper, #13) combines with Leo (The Sun, #19) to produce Jupiter (The Hierophant, #5). Hence, transformation of self is always an expansive process.

Aries 25°-27½° *Virgo:*
This segment is a careful and discerning planner. It has the mentality of a chess master. It often moves in a manner which will open up a particularly desired set of possibilities in the most efficient way possible. It is careful to protect its own personal interests.

This segment displays a flair for giving intelligent advice. It learns through copying or mimicking other people, but wants to carry out its work in its own personal manner rather than using methods dictated by someone else. It learns much from its past experience and will not jump into things without careful thought. It is a detailed critic, and is willing to take an active part in changing things, rather than passively pointing out faults.

It is capable of pitting a negative force against itself, or pitting two different negative forces against each other so that they will wreck mutual destruction. It knows that everything in existence has a wide variety of uses, and can turn curses into blessings just by the manner in which it deals with them.

It is a potential master at estimating the complete ramifications of a certain action and is aware that a certain action is only ideal at a certain time: that time being when its beneficial or desired effects most greatly outweigh its adverse reprecussions. Because of this, it is a natural pragmatist.

It must avoid its most natural pitfall: blind selfishness. It is so successful in maneuvering through the unexpected that there is danger of spiritual stagnation. When fully evolved, it becomes a well-spring of protection for the weak and needy.

The Tarot: Aries (The Reaper #13) combines with Virgo (Veiled Isis #2) to produce Saturn (The Black Magician #15). Hence, transformation of relative reality creates new structures and foundations, and therefore also changes one's fate.

Aries 27½°-30° *Libra:*

This segment is an instrument of activity. It believes that the best time to do something is now, and that once an idea has been conceived it should be put into effect immediately. It never wants to sit back and wait, but to get on with the business of living in the present.

It thinks of things in wholes, and because it can envision its goal, can keep moving toward it. It may take the attitude that the ends justify the means. It is a forcer of issues, and does not put much stock in abstractions.

It finishes things quickly and functions best in any activity where the returns are immediate.

It likes to do things with other people on a basis of equality. It needs to be able to express itself and will feel more secure when it is working in partnership.

It pushes other people, and seems to know intuitively just how far it can push. It has a talent for knowing the right time to do things. It can control others while appearing to be compromising.

It is adept at dispensing with trivia and cutting through great thicknesses of material to get to the heart of a matter.

It forces issues rather than waiting for them to take their course and would rather cause trouble now and get it over with than let problems grow.

The Tarot: Aries, (The Reaper, #13), combines with Libra, (Isis Unveiled, #3), to produce Mars, (The Lightning, #16). Hence, actively seeking transformation will prove beneficial since it will purify by destroying what is no longer necessary.

Taurus 0°-2½° *Libra:*

This segment is the natural healer. It strives to repair the old and worn out, and to rebuild what has broken down. It is friendly and benevolent in its approach to others. It develops strong, deep feelings

54

about its friends and once a friendship has been formed it will go to great lengths to maintain it. This is the segment of *giving and receiving*.

Negatively it may be meddlesome and take the attitude that it always knows best.

It tries to live what it believes, and to rationalize actions so they coincide with its moral code.

It wants to maintain a smooth and easy flow in its everyday life. It experiments with things, and likes to mix and combine energies around itself to see what their effect will be. It loves to try new methods and to invent new techniques.

It loves balance and harmony, combined with movement. It needs close associations, and wants to be influenced by others. It is happiest when experiencing a large amount of give and take in a relationship. Its creative and procreative urges are potent. It feels compelled to production, and likes to work in close conjunction with others. The act of creation usually has a rejuvenating rather than a draining effect.

The Tarot: Taurus, (The Alchemist, #14), combines with Libra, (Isis Unveiled, #3), to produce Gemini, (The Star, #17). Hence, powers of regeneration, put into action, produce hope and attract powerful and benign energies. (God helps those who help themselves).

Taurus 2½°-5° *Scorpio:*

This segment is naturally intuitive. It is capable of being in close touch with its own subconscious. It often feels sure of something which proves to be true.

It may have trouble relating to other people because it is naturally introverted. It learns most naturally from itself and is more interested in education as a refining of the senses than as a collecting of factual material from outside itself. It needs quiet solitude so that it may explore itself. Often when it becomes sick its illness can be traced directly to psychosomatic causes. It tends to experience psychic irritations thru the physical. Its bodily malfunctions are often difficult to diagnose. It responds to subtle treatments such as massage, homeopathy, hydrotherapy, and acupuncture.

Its energy operates at a moderate pace, but surely and with staying power.

This segment has a driving urge to know more about itself, and to get back to its own roots. It is not easily swayed by the advice or opinions of others and likes to try things independently so that it can see for itself.

Its creativity operates in spurts and generally centers around putting old ideas together in a new way rather than coming up with anything completely new.

It wants complete self control and feels it must contact all of its inner forces in order to know with what it is dealing. Its deepest need is to take command of its resources.

The Tarot: Taurus, (The Alchemist, #14), combines with Scorpio, (The Sovereign, #4), to produce Cancer, (The Moon, #18). Hence regeneration is a process of being attentive to the astral level. Successfully applied it can then overcome the deception of sickness and death.

Taurus 5°-7½° *Sagittarius:*
This is one of the most solid and stable segments of

Taurus. It is non-combative and will encounter adversity with passive resistance. It solves problems by attacking their cause rather than their symptoms.

It is willing to grow and change, but will always do so step by step rather than by rushing into things. It is effective in dealing with itself and can always learn by introspection and use what it learns to protect itself and further its own development.

It is highly moralistic and desirious of living up to its own codes. It is not dogmatic, but it will not change its mind unless it has sufficient reason. It is a slow but certain mover, and capable of exerting great will-power.

It successfully uses old methods and can bring a feeling of newness to ideas that are standard and established.

It is a natural master of the art of implication. It can create a particular aura which cannot be logically accounted for.

At its most unevolved, it is a blind upholder of the status quo, and will stubbornly stand in the way of genuine progress. Its rationalization of this will be that things are happening too fast. It must beware of a blinding suspicion of anything new.

The Tarot: Taurus, (The Alchemist, #14), combines with Sagittarius, (The Conquerer, #7), to produce the Sun, (The Adapt, #21). Hence rejuvenation of life is the process of understanding the domination of mind over matter. When this power has been mastered in both its theoretical and practical aspects, perfection has been achieved.

Taurus 7½°-10° *Capricorn:*

A stubborn and indominatable segment. At worst,

an unmitigated refusal to progress, at best an untouchably pure and powerful being who is a protector of things worth while to humanity.

This segment knows how to defend and sustain its assets. It looks for practical application for its personal resources. It may have a tendency to hoard.

A unique blend of the material and spiritual resides here. It wants to develop spiritually without forsaking or renouncing its physical possessions.

It tries to perfect its life-style by bringing its divergent interests into a finer and finer state of balance. It isn't content to take things as they are, but strives for more.

It can be self-justifying and pleasure-loving. It yearns for security that is unshakable and far-reaching. It does not get bored easily and can work happily within the limits of a tight routine as long as it is interested in the work.

It can develop fixations and wear itself out contemplating some single goal. It is capable of devoting all its energies to one end, and of centering every facet of its life around this end.

The Tarot: Taurus, (The Alchemist, #14) combines with Capricorn, (The Balance, #8), to produce Pluto, (The Materialist, #22). Hence, regeneration, when it becomes complete (crystallized) is a source of infinite spiritual power. It then becomes an automatic and eternal process which is built into the individual entity.

Taurus 10°-12½° *Aquarius:*

This segment has a clear and incisive vision. It is interested in processes and techniques and understanding things in detail. It is a natural repair man. It

58

tends to value friends and associates for what they know.

This segment has a lot of style and is generally quite ingratiating in its personal manner.

Experimenting and rearranging things for varied effect is natural and much can be achieved when working with limited materials. It is adept at making the best of what it has: a little can be made to seem like a lot. A love of crafts and handiwork is often indicated.

It is not wasteful in any sense, and appreciates economy on all levels, whether it be material or even intellectual. It can come directly to the point and express with simple clarity. It wants to see energy used effectively and resources spent in furthering a worthwhile goal.

It operates on an intuitive level and can grasp almost anything if given the time for direct experience with it. It is self-reliant and operates best when left alone in full charge of a task. It is good at envisioning the goal to be achieved.

Innocently candid in its self-expression, it will often learn from itself by analyzing what it has said or done.

The Tarot: Taurus, (The Alchemist, #14), combines with Aquarius, (The Sage, #9), to produce Jupiter, (The Hierophant, #5). Hence, regeneration, coupled with true wisdom, expands constantly, until it eventually takes in the whole of creation. Having repeatedly experienced the perpetual movement of life, the individual entity may then cognize the means by which to utilize the laws of nature for the highest good.

Taurus 12½°-15° *Pisces:*

This segment is a champion of causes. It attempts to maintain the basic doctrines of whatever movement it becomes associated with. It should try to give freely of itself in a transcendently generous manner. It overcomes difficulties through strong endurance. It is not egotistical. It tends to be more set in its beliefs than it appears. It often feels compelled to commit itself to a dogma.

This segment tends to protect itself from hurt in a love relationship, but it is anxious for an open intimacy, and when its confidence is gained, it can become extremely close to another person. Disappointments which come through friends often deepen its understanding of human nature. It does not give up friendships.

This segment is quite feminine in its staunch devotion. It does not like to see things come to an end. At worst, it can have problems in making changes in life.

There may be a compelling urge to do things, and to fulfill desires which go against its morality or common sense.

When it believes in an idea, its acceptance is immoveable. It may overjustify itself in an attempt to feel it is doing right. There is a dislike of being hemmed in or dictated to by others. This segment wants to give, but of its own accord.

It should beware of becoming "hung up" with possessions.

The Tarot: Taurus, (The Alchemist, #14), combines with Pisces, (The Martyr, #12), to produce Capricorn, (The Balance, #8). Hence, regeneration, which is worked for in the spirit of devotion, will eventually lead to universal equilibrium.

Taurus 15°-17½° *Aries:*

The primary function of Taurus is to maintain steadiness through readjustment of its energies and drives. Here it attempts new things periodically as a change of pace, usually returning to the old and familiar which is then seen in a new light. It doesn't give up, but is ever ready to start again. This segment likes long projects and challenging problems, and will work until they have been successfully coped with.

It is profoundly affected by environment and needs to avoid locations that may have an adverse effect. Often it is not aware of the powerful effect of its environment. It is a great lover of home and needs pleasant harmonious surroundings, especially if it is going to express creatively.

It can be outspoken. Its urge to express itself is nearly irrepressible and it may irritate others by its bluntness. It is a natural leader with strong paternalistic drives.

The Tarot: Taurus, (The Alchemist, #14), combines with Aries, (The Reaper, #13), to produce Aquarius, (The Sage, #9). Hence regeneration is not merely a replacing of parts which restore, but an evolutionary process which raises the vibration of what it heals. This process is like a spiral rather than a circle, and it leads inward to a source of infinite wisdom.

Taurus 17½°-20° *Taurus:*

This segment experiments and invents. It is an artist who searches for new modes of self-expression. It is egocentric, but usually in a life-supporting manner. Its creative attempts are typically direct and uninhibited.

At best, it functions as a physician in the highest sense of the word. It has a built-in knowledge of psychic healing. Unlike a doctor who is versed only in exoteric healings, it can often produce remedies which are effective because they cure more perfectly than generally accepted scientific methods.

This segment experiences sudden turns of fate stemming from a hidden source within itself. It can manifest sudden illnesses either mental or physical, which seem impossible to diagnose or cure, but can also take unexpected turns for the better. Its most developed trait is stamina.

As an artist, this segment could well turn into a megalomanic. On the positive side, it sees art as a high mission to which it will dedicate itself with priestly reverence. It can turn any line of work into an "artistic experience."

This segment is influenced by its frequent dreams. This is a characteristic manifestation of the powerful energy source which lies beneath its conscious mind, and which will periodically send forth vivid flashes.

The Tarot: Taurus, (The Alchemist, #14), combines with Taurus, (The Alchemist, #14), to produce Uranus, (The Wheel, #10). Hence, regeneration is a miracle totally dependant on fate, (Hell), or divine intervention, (Heaven).

Taurus 20°-22½° *Gemini:*

This segment may have difficulty making decisions because it tends to collect more information than it needs. It is concerned with how to spend its time and resources. It wants to use these resources where they will do the most good.

At best, this is one of the most flexible segments of the zodiac, in that it maintains its Taurean stability while being resiliant enough to bend with adversity. It is resourceful in its methods and can give up when it sees that a certain line of endeavor is not going to work. It may give up a certain plan of attack, but it will never give up the fight. It knows that there is more than one way to overcome problems.

It is passive but persistent and may attempt to get what it wants by devious means. On the surface it can seem agreeable when it is actually stubborn and stolid.

This segment is optimistic because it has strong faith that it is capable of doing anything. It feel that anything which has been lost can be retrieved.

It is not easy to understand this segment because it is careful to cover its true nature. It must avoid trying to make itself appear good in the eyes of others while forsaking its actual self.

The Tarot: Taurus (The Alchemist, #14) combines with Gemini (The Star, #17) to produce Scorpio (The Sovereign, #4). Hence, regeneration is a source of hope for the future and faith in universal integrity. When this hope and faith are possessed, help comes from higher levels to further realization.

Taurus 22½°-25° *Cancer:*

This segment functions in a subjective manner. It has difficulty verbalizing and objectifying ideas. It is naturally introverted and needs time to be alone. It has a strong potential for mediumship.

It is one of the most solitary segments of the zodiac, and wants to be completely independent. It is resourceful and can fall back on itself when outside help fails.

It is often more psychic than it thinks and can be peculiarly affected by people and surroundings. Often it will rationalize these odd effects away and therefore be unaware of real reasons behind events. Self-deception is easy. Positively it can evolve through a closer attentiveness to its own emotions and subconscious functioning. It needs to avoid making snap judgements. It may tend to play unconscious tricks on itself by confusing hunches with personal bias. It senses danger readily, but will often jam the signals of a clear broadcast by applying logic to feeling. It needs to learn to wait, listen, and be silent, and it is through this that it will avoid a chaotic mental state and be able to use itself as a resource for channelling energy from the collective unconscious.

The Tarot: Taurus (The Alchemist, #14) combines with Cancer (The Moon, #18), to produce Jupiter, (The Hierophant, #5). Hence, regeneration is a process of breaking up stress — relaxing and stilling the mind so that the natural force of evolution can take its course. This produces expansion of self.

Taurus 25°-27½° *Leo*:

Perfection is the goal of this segment. It seeks a limitless field in which to work, and requires challenging goals to spur it onward. It is idealistic and can overlook a flaw of the moment to see its future achievement. It is a hard worker, and has amazing willpower.

It is bent on fulfilling its dreams. Seeds that are planted when young are often nurtured throughout the life.

It is mystified by itself and delights in the workings of its own mind. It may be self-willed. The creative urge is as primordial as nature itself. This segment enjoys making things and putting things together. The fruits of its endeavors will convey the stamp of the creator's hand.

This segment desires to expose its uniqueness. It finds it nearly impossible to cater to others in a superficial manner.

Here is a great love of home and a tendency to identify strongly with possessions. Usually there will be a great flourish of eccentricity towards the end of life.

The Tarot: Taurus (The Alchemist, #14) combines with Leo (The Sun, #19) to produce Venus (The Two Paths, #6). Hence, regeneration is the joyous process of the individual coming into closer union with the absolute. This is assured because it will not be content with anything less than perfection.

Taurus 27½°-30° *Virgo:*

A love of learning techniques and procedures which are practical typifies this segment. It is often drawn toward mysticism. It is one of the most inquisitive segments of the zodiac. It wants to use what it knows and experiments to find newer and better modes of doing things. It operates best under highly disciplined conditions.

It is adept at finding the flaws in a system. It knows how to make things run smoothly. Its forte is being persuasive. By whatever means it uses, it is likely to have many people agreeing with it. It knows how to dramatize both the pros and cons of an issue. Its morality is usually subjective, in that it lives by rules but provides generously for exceptions.

It is appreciative of help from others and likes to work with them toward a common goal. It needs a situation where it can either take orders from someone more knowledgeable than itself, or give orders to someone who plays the role of apprentice or student. The reason for this is that its vision is so personal that a joint effort based on complete equality is well-nigh impossible. A definite division of labor is what is needed.

The Tarot: Taurus (The Alchemist, #14) combines with Virgo (Veiled Ises, #2) to produce Mars (The Lightning, #16) Hence, regeneration approached scientifically and based on the secrets of nature reveal the way out of adversity.

Gemini 0°-2½° *Virgo:*

This segment has an acute understanding of the dichotomy between appearance and reality. Its mind operates in a factual and detailed manner. It may tend to collect more information than it can adequately deal with. At best it is a precise thinker and communicator.

Gemini is the sign of hope. It is the most dualistic sign of the zodiac, and it is just this dualistic quality which makes evolution possible. This first segment of Gemini is cognizant of the double meaning inherent in all things. For this reason it may have difficulty making choices. An antidote for this is to put things into a larger and ever-expanding context so that a better estimation of a situation could be made, rather than indulging in mental nit-picking.

This is one of the sharpest segments for mental pursuits. It can put its finger an ambiguity with crystal-clear surety. It usually loves mental exertion.

Karmically, it must beware of learning tricks which hold it at a particular level and keep it from evolving. The mind here is subtle and feminine in its approach. Often it is indirect in expression, and has a natural bent for rhetoric.

An optomistic set of mind is in evidence also, because a riddle is always seen by this segment as a challenge, something to be solved. It never admits to the existence of a valid question which has no answer.

The Tarot: Gemini, (The Star, #17), combines with Virgo, (Veiled Isis, #2), to produce Leo, (The Sun, #19). Hence, illusion covers the truth. Mystery approached with faith in the potential of its unveiling can result in satisfaction.

Gemini 2½°-5° *Libra:*

This is the most active segment of Gemini. It is more satisfied when busy. Movement here is solely for the sake of movement. A positive set mind keeps this segment from ever winding down. It can achieve unexpected results just by laboring long enough. It is unhesitating and persistent and can gain the confidence of others by seeming to know exactly what it is doing. It asks a lot of questions and will approach a situation from many angles at once. It wants the opin-

67

ions of a wide variety of people. Negatively, it should avoid "spinning its wheels."

It is aware of the infinite number of possible connections between things, and that these connections supply never-ending possibilities for action. This makes escape from danger always possible, and if a course of action cannot be plotted, then one thing after another may be tried in a process of trial and error until the proper route is found.

This segment may be unable to complete things or, at the opposite extreme, goes too far on a project and thereby ruins it after completion. It sees everything as in a process of gestation and therefore is in danger of not realizing the birth when it happens.

At best it is candidly itself and will act immediately on what it believes.

The Tarot: Gemini (The Star, #17) combines with Libra (Isis Unveiled, #3), to produce the Moon, (The Sarcophagus, #20). Hence, faith and hope, when put into action can effect a reawakening of consciousness and a resurrection of what was thought to be lost.

Gemini 5°-7½° *Scorpio:*

This segment's awareness operates suddenly and will experience quick flashes of the wholeness of reality. The mind is erratic and disjunctive in its movements. Here Gemini's dualism has the power to become simultaneous — effectively combined at a point which transends the polarity of opposites.

Air is the ordering and connective principle, and here Gemini's airy nature has the power to organize information in a manner which will make it most effective.

68

This segment symbolizes those points of transition between dualities where neither one nor the other is in effect. What lies at these points is nothingness — the absolute, and it is here that the potential to rise above opposites lies.

This segment can be a master of ambiguity. It can so confuse the difference between the real and the seeming that something more than either is created.

It will love to talk but probably has a difficult time explaining itself because it seeks to communicate the subtlest and most ineffable insights that it has. It is a natural poet because it is forced to explain itself through metaphor. Its challenge is to control and direct its powers of thinking and communicating.

It feels truth as something everpresent in an ideal sense, but something which becomes relative when objectified.

A highly gifted scientist as well as a poet might have this segment emphasized — since there is no difference between the two.

The Tarot: Gemini, (The Star, #17), combines with Scorpio, (The Sovereign, #14), to produce the Sun, (The Adept, #21). Hence, hope realized leads to perfection, and truth experienced completely is life's goal.

Gemini 7½°-10° *Sagittarius:*

Here is pure delight in exerting the mind. This segment is concerned with methods to dominate natural forces. It sees the mind as ruler of matter and wants to harness material resources so that they may be used to their fullest potential. It is a master of using disguises as a means of getting desired results through trickery. (An example of this could be a doctor who cures patients with sugar pills because he knows the malady is psychosomatic and can gain the patient's confidence). It is more interested in speaking to achieve a desired effect than it is in speaking to express openly what it thinks. It is good at talking to others on their own level and in their own terms. At worst, this amounts to condescending.

There is often a love of studying religions. The beliefs are usually broad and liberal. There is little interest in morality as an abstraction. It bases its judgements of actions on whether or not the actions are effective, rather than if they are good or evil.

This segment feels more secure when it is well-educated, and may manifest a fear of people who know more than it does.

It needs to anchor itself to a meaningful basis for existence, and learn to love in a universal sense, so that its powers do not disintegrate into mere intellectual guile and chicanery.

The Tarot: Gemini (The Star, #17) combines with Sagittarius (The Conquerer, #7), to produce Venus (The Two Paths, #6). Hence, truth is the prime weapon of the Conquerer, but he must beware of the temptation to use it negatively.

Gemini 10°-12½° *Capricorn:*

Here is an unshakeable confidence. The dualistic nature of Gemini is used here to achieve practical ends. The mind is usually certain of what it wants and can stick to a goal more one-pointedly than Gemini is usually thought capable of. It ignores outside influence and can be oblivious of anything which does not concern it. It may be thought of by others as being cold and unfeeling. It is capable of being logical and clear in its thinking. It has a knack for being able to dispense with the unnecessary, and has a genius for saying much with few words.

Negatively, its mind may lack originality. It makes few mistakes, and therefore is not prone to those fortunate accidents of discovery through which great leaps in progress are made. At best, it adds competent and well-thought-out knowledge to some established field, and is tuned-into the usability of ideas.

It can be very spiritual without ever concerning itself openly with spiritual matters. It may even dislike anything which smacks of religion and is not interested in what could be — only in what is. It may be derisive of idealism because it champions action over intention.

The mind-body coordination is usually well-developed, and hence many performers are apt to be found here.

As an occultist, this segment will excel since it will use its knowledge as a direct medium of assistance, rather than becoming bound up with ideas which cannot be workably applied.

The Tarot: Gemini (The Star, #17) combines with Capricorn (The Balance, #8) to produce Sagittarius (The Conquerer, #7). Hence, truth which can be crystallized is ultimate power. Hope which is right action, (in line with the Prime Force), will be fulfilled.

Gemini 12½°-15° *Aquarius:*

The unattached nature of this segment makes it capable of seeing things as they truly are. It is a penetrator of appearances. Its natural function is to give advice or be a consultant because it makes the

71

most of its experiences in terms of learning from them. It is capable of removing itself completely from a situation so that it may obtain a complete picture of what is going on. It has great respect for wisdom and education. It is always in the process of learning and knows that everything that happens has a personal meaning. It is a good listener.

It is also quite effective at getting along with and relating to a wide variety of people. There is little problem here with either inferiority or superiority complexes.

Limitations are a challenge to this segment. It is happy to work within bounds and will try to do its best with what it has.

It avoids passing judgement on things from some rigid viewpoint, and is always willing to accept its notions as its own, rather than forcing them on others. It sees its way of life as a result of what has happened to it, and knows that other modes of existence can also be valid and meaningful.

It senses that everyone is potentially wise in his own right and that truth has manifold expressions.

It loves to experiment with ideas.

The Tarot: Gemini (The Star, #17) combines with Aquarius (The Sage, #9), to produce Capricorn (The Balance, #8). Hence, when the inner light of hope is coupled with knowledge gleaned from experience, one's personal karma is accepted as a necessary instrument of development.

Gemini 15°-17½° *Pisces:*

Gemini is commonly thought to rule the mind, and here it is at its most intuitive and subjective. This segment is illogical, yet it can approach correct con-

72

clusions by "feeling" its way to them. It is adamant and forceful in its thinking and is difficult to reason with when it is convinced.

Realizing that relative reality is a constant battle of opposing forces, and that relative truth is a two-edged sword, it can be arbitrary in its dicisions. It knows that the ability to make choices is, in itself, an illusion.

It receives strong and quick impressions and is highly capable of what C. C. Zain calls, "intellectual divination" — that is, reading personality through seemingly aimless free-association.

Negatively, it may be misinformed, and tend to distort information toward what it feels to be true. It is not in the least timid and can relate to others in a frank and uninhibited manner.

It can effectively overcome impasses since it does not meet them rationally, and is difficult to outwit because it does not think in a step-by-step process.

It often shows great sympathy for those who are not well-off and can be a dedicated social worker. It feels a sense of duty to search for and fulfill its mission in life.

Its personal magnetism can be extreme.

The Tarot: Gemini, (The Star, #17), combines with Pisces, (The Martyr, #12), to produce Neptune, (The Enchantress, #11). Hence, when truth is sacrificed to, and faith in the universal law is strong, then great force and spiritual power are generated.

Gemini 17½°-20° *Aries:*

This is a high-activity segment. Much labor will be found here, as well as a functioning which is liquid, changeable and forever starting new projects. Decisions are quickly made and work is carried out with

73

lightening speed. The body may have difficulty keeping up with the mind, and overexertion through incessant thinking is possible.

This segment needs to learn discipline and a narrower channeling of its energies so that it can go farther in one direction rather than dispersing its power for only short distances in a multitude of ways.

It has the potential of instilling hope in others and giving them direction. Its exhuberance is infectious.

It needs to always feel that it is accomplishing something, and should not look at the work it has to do as a vast task, but take things step-by-step. It may worry too much about the future.

Much depends upon the thoughts. This segment can do almost anything it thinks it can. It may experience swiftly alternating cycles of upliftment and depression. It can think itself into either success or failure. As long as it thinks there is a means by which to fulfill its desires, it can work without stopping. If it is sure of itself in its own mind, it will try something again and again until it triumphs.

This segment signifies "freshness of ideas."

The Tarot: Gemini (The Star, #17) combines with Aries (The Reaper, #13) to produce Libra (Ises Unveiled, #3). Hence, hope when constantly renewed will trigger action, which is in turn always productive. Faith in the constant newness of all things impels another cycle of birth.

Gemini 20°-22½° *Taurus:*

This segment is original and experimental in a deliberate and organized manner. It can have a sustaining influence on everything around it. It loves to play with ideas — re-combing them to discover new truths.

74

Here Gemini is most logical and structured in its thinking. It still moves swiftly, but doesn't run away with itself or get out of hand. The movements are secure. Fact and feet are kept on the ground. Insanity is not probable — but if derangement occurs, it can be difficult to cure.

This segment is quieter than most other segments of Gemini, and when it speaks, it does not mince words. Forethought in communication is in evidence. It tends to pattern and systemize its thinking. Linguistic stylists might have this segment emphasized in their charts.

An understanding of blueprints, designs and plans is indicated. Artisticly, this segment will function more on a rational than on an intuitive level. It will objectify its ideas and spend much time at the drawing board rather than laying heavy emphasis on the act of creation.

Knowledge and information are treated as resources. Often this segment will put on airs in a satirical manner; it learns by imagining roles and then playing them, sometimes in a fantastic manner and sometimes seriously.

The Tarot: Gemini (The Star, #17) combines with Taurus (The Alchemist, #14) to produce Scorpio (The Sovereign, #4). Hence duality is at the service of the self. Everything has its purpose in the universal scheme, and to combine polar opposites in the most life-supporting manner produces realization.

Gemini 22½°-25° *Gemini:*

This segment is fast and without reservation it its self-expression. It receives many impressions which come and go swiftly. It may have difficulty in catching ideas in a meaningful sequence and following them because its attention is easily diverted. The tongue is sharp and fast and the coordination is excellent. Many mental connections are made between things in a somewhat obsessive manner. There is a tendency to think out loud.

This segment likes to move around alot and can be uncontrollably nervous. It likes a smoothly-run environment, with everything in its place, not because it worships order, but for the sake of convenience. It can't bear losing things or having to wait. It finds boredom intolerable.

The attention is one-pointed, though momentary.

There is a strong urge here to follow the self and to listen to the workings of one interior being to the exclusion of all outside static. This segment needs to make up its mind for itself. It can be self-willed, although not in a defensive manner. It merely tunes out those forces which attempt to compel it to do something it does not want to do.

Since every man is a potential God, it knows that there is no reason for leaders and followers, in the sense of masters who dictate unquestionable policy to slaves.

The most worthy thing this segment can do is to be totally itself without worrying about criticism.

The Tarot: Gemini (The Star, #17) combines with Gemini (The Star, #17), to produce Sagittarius (The Conquerer, #7). Hence, hope which is not merely intellectual, but which is vivified by the interior flame which illuminates the self, can achieve victory over anything.

Gemini 25°-27½° *Cancer:*

This segment could be called the most anti-social of Gemini. Its functioning is interiorized and intro-verted. It nurtures ideas and mulls over thoughts without exposing many of its mental processes. Its intellectual functioning is partially submerged in its subconscious mind, and its thinking is powered by emotional force. It communicates best through symbol and metaphor.

It usually develops its thoughts over a long period of time.

It is an excellent mimic. It can copy the styles of others with ease and can learn much by accurately reproducing things which it has seen before. There is a mischieviousness here, which, at worst, is satanic. This segment can make appearance and reality change place, or it can clairify the difference between the two.

This segment is quick to see and understand the nature of deceptions. It likes to figure puzzles and solve mysteries. It is fascinated by illusions.

It is intrigued by danger rather than afraid. It is curious about itself and would rather explore its own depths than never know what lurks inside itself. Its faith in its own eternal nature frees it from a fear of annihilation. Its stability may be hidden, but it is solid as rock.

We might title this segment "The Gardener of Ideas."

The Tarot: Gemini, (The Star, #17), combines with Cancer, (The Moon, #18), to produce Capricorn, (The Balance, #8). Hence, the interior light of man, when it braves the abyss of the unknown, becomes strong, tempered, and crystallized. Faith meets its challenge and is judged.

Gemini 27½°-30° *Leo:*

This segment is capable of extreme happiness. The mind is open and non-judgmental. It knows that there is always more to learn and is fascinated with the intricacy of the relative world. It rejoices in the ever-shifting nature of events and circumstances. It wants experience.

It is content to just be, and is willing to learn from any activity which is going on around it. It lives by Blake's dictum that, "energy is pure delight."

The sense of humor is well-developed. It will laugh at anything when it can, and it has a unique sense of removal from tragedy because it knows that all things must pass, including catastrophes.

Negatively there is an utter lack of self-assertiveness. This segment is always getting ready to do something — rehearsing a part — but it may never get around to playing the actual role. It may suffer from a sense of lonliness, since it is always aware of the duality between itself and the rest of reality. There is a love of involvement, but a sense that the involvement is never complete enough.

A strong death wish is often present due to a desire for a closeness impossible to find on this plane of existence.

In old age this segment can produce a gentle but staunch sagacity.

The Tarot: Gemini, (The Star, #17) combines with Leo, (The Sun, #19), to produce Aquarius, (The Sage,

#9). Hence, the duality of creation, when participated in with fervor and exhuberance will lead to wisdom in the way of the world. To be happy in one's faith, and to let one's own light shine through, will, in the course of time, lead to wisdom.

Cancer 0°-2½° *Leo:*

This segment rejoices in the act of creating and nurturing. It needs to have ideals or someone in whom it sees its ideals. It wants to be a receptive servant of truth and knowledge.

It desires parenthood and loves to give birth to something which it can call its own. It can become attached to possessions, more for their sentimental value than for their intrinsic worth. It feels most secure and able to assert itself at home.

It is fascinated with the processes of growth and development. It yearns for closeness and can become deeply moved when in love. It may like emotionalism purely for its own sake and negatively can seek out adverse situations because of the emotional response evoked from them.

It can be moody. It will shift swiftly back and forth between the roles of parent and child. It listens with its feelings and will favor emotion over reason.

Pathologically, it may take the attitude that it is the only one that feels, or that its emotions are uniquely its own. It tends to dramatize its feelings.

The Tarot: Cancer, (The Moon, #18), combines with Leo, (The Sun, #19), to produce Uranus (The Wheel, #10). Hence, to give birth is an ecstatic experience at one time and a burden at another. Creation is the turning of fate which produces now joy and now pain.

Cancer 2½°-5° *Virgo:*

This segment has a 'feel' for science. It approaches knowledge intuitively, and can use what it knows effectively.

It is often interested in occultism. It wants to be pure, but how this will manifest in its personality in an individual sense is hard to say.

It is one of the most intensely emotional segments of the Zodiac, although it may keep much of this emotionalism under cover, especially when the emotion is sorrow. Minor details can elicit strong feelings.

It is often intent on physical cleanliness and health. It needs to dedicate itself to a cause, and when it does, it can be faithful to it.

It must beware of repressing its feelings. It can think that it has worked a problem out within itself and later find that the emotions have only been repressed. Finding an effective outlet for feelings can mean all the difference to its well being.

It can become desperately caught up in its own ambivalence, and must guard against turning its subconscious into its own worst enemy just because it does not want to admit to the existence of a particular feeling. It can often feel betrayed or inhibited by its own instincts.

This is the most passive segment of Cancer when it comes to dealing with others.

The Tarot: Cancer (The Moon, #18) combines with Virgo (Veiled Isis, #2) to produce the Moon (The Sarcophagus, #20). Hence, the mind's submission to the medium of physical body calls forth the feminine principle. The feeling nature of man is dualistic and its anima has the power to revive him.

Cancer 5°-7½° *Libra:*

This segment embodies that element of strength, power, and vitality which heightens and vivifies the feminine principle, making it even more feminine.

The cardinal, outgoing elements of Cancer are most in evidence in this segment. It likes to relate to other people and is quite opportunistic. It wants to play a well-defined role in a relationship.

It responds strongly to beauty and its aesthetic sense disregards the tragic and horrible, which are only acceptable to it if presented in a purely imaginary manner.

It would rather encounter people in its own home than outside. It is constantly seeking emotional equilibrium, and may see personal relationships as a source of security.

It senses the great depth of its personal power and this can give it a feeling of security. It will work diligently to use and develop its talents and potentials.

It can display much emotional control without suppressing or injuring its feelings. If it can't let a motive manifest in one way, then it will actively find another.

Its most exalted feature is an ability to wish something so strongly that it comes true. It can project its self-image so intensely that it can become what it is projecting. For this reason it must avoid negative thoughts, because their effect could be catastrophic.

The Tarot: Cancer, (The Moon, #18), combines with Libra, (Isis Unveiled, #3), to produce the Sun, (The Adept, #21). Hence, the feeling body of man becomes powerful and activated. It unites with the will to produce the highest possible human perfection. The subconscious, through knowledge gained from finer and finer states of activity, can finally unite completely with the conscious.

Cancer 7½°-10° *Scorpio:*

The emotions here are amazingly acute. The body awareness is powerful enough to produce insanity if an unhealthy interest in it develops. Negative emotional states can be directly caused by subtle physical malfunctions.

This segment needs physical discipline. Dance, yoga, or any form of exercise has a balancing effect. It is an astute judge of its potential and capabilities, and would make a good doctor, masseuse or chiropractor. It has a feel for the bodies of others as well as its own. Its powers of recuperation are strong.

Whether it is aware of it or not, it is in close contact with the astral world, and will often feel emotions and impressions which seem irrational because they are not obviously linked with physical reality. It is a good judge of character but may tend to dismiss impressions because it cannot find logical reasons for them. It is capable of being inspired by entities on the astral plane who may try to communicate. This is why it must keep its body finely tuned — so that it will be more receptive to positive astral influence and less subject to the negative ones.

It should watch the diet and avoid drugs. The sex drive here is often quite intense.

At its most developed, this segment can exercise amazing control over itself and other people through its thoughts. When put to positive use this ability can be used for psychic healing.

The Tarot: Cancer, (The Moon, #18), combines with

Scorpio, (The Sovereign, #4), to produce Pluto, (The Materialist, #22). Hence, the feeling body of man becomes realized to produce great power because it taps the force of evolution. The senses, raised to total sentience, produce infinite creative energy.

Cancer 10°-12½° *Sagittarius:*

This segment has a strong emotional need for religious beliefs. It can become upset when its philosophy of life does not explain outer events.

It longs for perfect security and hence attempts to reject gross forms of protection, such as money and possessions, in favor of relying more and more upon itself. This does not imply that it will not work to accumulate money; it means that it desires to extricate itself from those things in life which it cannot be absolutely sure of. It fears dependence of any sort, and can renounce something which it dearly loves to prove to itself that it can function with the barest necessities.

It is excellent at taking care of other people and making them comfortable. It loves large families and emotional security usually comes late in life. Travelling is a great stimulus to its imagination.

It wants to understand itself, and therefore can become confused or anxious by extensions of itself. It wants to make sure that its extensions truly reflect what it feels itself to be. It can show dedication in a highly self-assertive manner when it senses itself becoming confused or over-shadowed.

Its soul is strong and needs to be able to co-exist with the rest of life without being annihilated through being misunderstood or taken for granted.

The Tarot: Cancer, (The Moon, #18), combines with Sagittarius, (The Conquerer, #7), to produce Sagittarius, (The Conquerer, #7). Hence, the feeling body of man is capable of dominating matter. Its power to do this is tested, and it will be victorious.

Cancer 12½°-15° *Capricorn:*

This is the most fearless segment of Cancer. It has great emotional control, and is capable of avoiding personal relationships when it sees them as being impractical. Its constitution is exceptionally strong.

It works ideas of which it is sure and rejects others. It is independent. Negatively it can be over-opinionated, but it is sure of its own stand on things.

Its mind is quite hard to change. It has to be careful of self-deception and thinking that because an impulse is powerful it is correct.

It is rarely confused by other people, but is often confused by itself. It is a natural critic and is not shy in revealing its personal bias.

The instincts are strong and can be a source of deception. This segment has difficulty dealing with its inner drives because they are so powerful. Negatively it tends to project itself heavily on other people, and can have trouble seeing others for what they really are.

Positively, it can know exactly what others need from it for their own personal development. This knowledge will become more and more in evidence as this segment works out its own karma. It must learn to not dwell upon itself. It can only receive love by first giving it.

The attractions and repulsions are usually intense

here and often deceptive. This segment may feel attracted to something which it later grows to hate, or vice versa.

The Tarot: Cancer (The Moon, #18) combines with Capricorn (The Balance, #8) to produce Capricorn (The Balance, #8). Hence, the feeling body of man presents a certain structure which the workings of karma will either preserve or tear down. Either way, the end result will be a new structure more in line with cosmic harmony.

Cancer 15°-17½° *Aquarius:*

This segment has trouble separating reason from emotion, but this can be turned into an asset. Through this it can gain insight into the source of its objectivity and rationale.

It has difficulty envisioning ends. Instead it views reality as an infinite progression. Cancer's expansion becomes an unbounded ideal through Aquarius. Cancer's sense of home becomes wholly subjective — identified with the universe itself.

This segment desires wisdom. Its curiosity often leads it into danger, and confuses it with more information than it can handle. On the other hand, it is saved by its caution which is strong enough to protect it, although not strong enough to keep it from self-exploration. It can sense danger, and will hold back and wait at times of impending disaster.

It takes a practical approach to knowledge. If it cannot use its knowledge for development, the information is discarded.

This segment enjoys communal living and will often play the role of a wise mother. It wants to expand and protect its community. It loves contact with new people and situations.

It needs acceptance for itself and may minimize conformity in order to be accepted.

The Tarot: Cancer (The Moon, #18) combines with Aquarius (The Sage, #9) to produce Aquarius (The Sage, #9). Hence, the astral plane is where wisdom is put on trial, and if it is strong enough to withstand this trial, it will emerge from the test unchanged.

Cancer 17½°-20° *Pisces:*

This is a hard-working and dedicated segment. It is capable of donating all to a cause. It has a compelling urge to serve, and does not bewail its fate. Its best quality is an ability to labor without reward. If it believes in something, it will act on principle. It can be one of the most giving segments of the Zodiac.

Its biggest danger is the tendency to devote its efforts to the wrong things. It is extreme in both its confidence and distrust of others. It is often too gullible and can be easily swayed by a good manipulator.

It may often feel that it is a slave to its own emotions and impulses, and can talk itself into the idea that it cannot control its drives. It can feel that it either needs to be dominated or needs to dominate someone else. It may worry about security.

There is a strong sense of duty to self present. The need to dedicate the life to a cause is a projection of this. This segment must beware of confusing altruism with pure selfishness, and also of manipulating others in an indirect and passive manner.

It will work out its stress in a manner similar to psychodrama. It is bent on expressing itself. A quality of being excessive and submerging itself deep within its neuroses can be the very instrument through which it achieves liberation.

The Tarot: Cancer (The Moon, #18) combines with Pisces (The Martyr, #12) to produce Libra (Isis Unveiled, #3). Hence, the feeling body of man encounters the natural laws of the universe. This produces action that can surmount destruction and proceed to creation on a higher plane.

Cancer 20°-22½° *Aries:*

This segment is not easily influenced by anything outside itself. It will often lead a private life and have a private circle of friends.

Its will to live and protect itself is hidden. It may seem weak, but functions excellently in crises situations. Its subconscious can go through transformations of which it is not aware. The transformation becomes clear in retrospect.

It tends to think for itself and will often become confused when others advise or try to help.

It is highly emotional and needs to feel things on this level before it can completely understand. It is good at picking up the pieces after a shattering experience.

It communicates in an emotional rather than logical manner. It can experience great inner conflict that will seem to have little to do with outside circumstances. It will often cover its motives and be secretive about its activities.

Its contentment depends on its state of mind. It has the potential to cope with almost anything, but a conscious decision to endure a situation may be vetoed by the subconscious mind. This is when problems set in.

It can seem to go through sudden and unbelievable personality changes. Others will often see only the end result of a long process of internal workings which have led to this dramatic metamorphasis of self.

The Tarot: Cancer (The Moon, #18) combines with Aries (The Reaper, #13) to produce Scorpio (The Sovereign, #4). Hence, the feeling body of man percieves its own transformation and through this attains self-realization.

Cancer 22½°-25° *Taurus:*

This segment loves to keep itself busy. It is always thinking, making plans, or carrying them out. It has a strong sense of order which is subjective. It needs to identify and organize ideas within itself. Often it will act out aggressions in its mind so vividly that it will not need to let them manifest in reality.

It loves stories, tales and fantasies. It wants to be impressed with feeling. It is sensuous, although much of its sensuality is apt to be relegated to daydreaming rather than to actual involvements.

As an artist it creates moods and speels. It can come up with unique combinations which are suggestive without being obvious. It has a feel for producing illusions. Its creations are borne out of intuition. Often it will mimic other forms, but is able to add a new twist. It likes to vary a theme.

This segment is in great need of emotional stability, and in a situation where this stability is interrupted, it will compensate uniquely for the imbalance it feels. It can be stubbornly defensive.

Often the sense of touch is highly developed which produces insight into the character of others based on their body language.

This segment needs a permanent form of security so it is led to working on its inner self. It organizes its resources so it will never be caught off guard. We might name it "constancy of feeling."

The Tarot: Cancer (The Moon, #18) combines with Taurus (The Alchemist, #14) to produce Jupiter (The Hierophant, #5). Hence, the feeling body of man, in its aspect of constant movement, produces alternate balance and imbalance. This causes spiritual expansion.

Cancer 25°-27½° *Gemini:*

Cancer is moody here. Emotions come and go rapidly. There is danger of confusing inner and outer perception, making it difficult at times for this segment to understand others, since it is inclined to project its feelings onto them. It can derive security from communicating with others.

This segment's insight is uneven. It can be naively ignorant of things which are obvious to others, and yet acutely perceptive of things less obvious. It can be gullible one minute and see through fallacy the next. Its manner of reasoning is far from objective because it relates everything to itself.

It is set in its ways and has an innocent fearlessness because it senses its immortal nature even through the deception of death. It can be egotistical, but in an easy and self-assured manner. It feels no need to prove its worth, since it is so completely self-assured.

Its attempts at being productive or generous are often for the purpose of receiving adulation or love.

It desires direct intimacy and respects truthfulness in others.

Its emotional ambivalance should not be contained, because this will cause stress. It must learn to express feelings so that negative impulses will not produce inward tension.

The Tarot: Cancer (The Moon, #18) combines with Gemini (The Star, #17) to produce Capricorn (The Balance, #8). Hence, the feeling body of man experiences the dualism between appearance and reality. He may then bring these forces into a state of equilibrium within himself.

Cancer 27½°-30° *Cancer:*

This segment may have an aggressive and enterprising exterior, but is actually a private type. It takes time to understand it. It is usually not talkative and will retreat from situations it feels it cannot handle.

It slips easily into semiconscious states of awareness such as daydreams, fantasy, etc. Its childhood is usually emotionally intense.

To those who are close to it, it will seem like a certain part of it is somehow removed and unaccessable. It may feel very much alone in the world, but is not inclined to feel lonely. It wants intimacy and companionship but can develop a feeling of claustrophobia if it is not allowed an occassional retreat into itself. It is very tuned-in to "atmospheres" and "ambience."

It appears to others at once very young and very old. There is a quality of innocence coupled with understanding.

Often it cannot account for its actions, except to itself. This is due to an inability to explain things in a manner which would be understood by others. (The Medieval Astrologers referred to Cancer as a "mute sign").

Its interior world is usually more developed than its exterior world. It may play the role of the absent-minded professor who pays so much attention to the subjective workings of his own inner being that he is oblivious of the superficial goings on around him.

The Tarot: Cancer (The Moon, #18) combines with Cancer (The Moon, #18) to produce Aquarius (The Sage, #9). Hence, the feeling body of man is his connective link with the astral world. The purpose of this feeling body is to recieve and transmit wisdom.

Leo 0°-2½° *Cancer:*

The initial segment of Leo is the first awareness of the sanctity of self. This segment protects its individuality, is defensive about its right to be autonomous, and is often uncompromising. It treats itself as its own parent rather than looking to others for this type of guidance. It is proud of any ability it has, and is anxious to show its worth.

This segment is a natural performer. It has to learn to conquer the fluxuation of feeling now superior and now inferior. It needs to be accepted for its goodness, rather than for its potential performance or ability.

As a child it can act rebelliously and as a parent it can play childish games with its own child. It is a compulsive competitor, but will often experience a feeling of emptiness after a victory. It can be self-critical, but does not take criticism from others well. A masculine demeanor hides a feminine emotional makeup. This segment tries to test the worth of those in a position of power and authority. It will aggressively defend the rights of others. When feeling insecure, it may hide behind a facade of self-assurance.

It may take an unhealthy delight in its own shortcomings as a means of daring others to attempt to censure it.

At best it is protective of creative effort. It is concerned with its own self image and wants to be thought magnanimous.

The Tarot: Leo (The Sun, #19) combines with Cancer (The Moon, #18) to produce Uranus (The Wheel, #10). Hence, joy and happiness produce a sudden awakening to the truths of reality. The individual desires to stand alone so that he may be tested by fate. (The Wheel of Fortune).

Leo 2½°-5° *Leo:*

This segment symbolizes the magic of selfhood. It is highly dramatic in its mode of functioning. It has natural sense of its own presence in all situations. It can be generous, although it should not expect anything in return.

It can display a prideful arrogance which is due to self-exaltation rather than to putting others down. It is a passionate lover. It is easily angered, although it does not stay angry. Its vitality is usually strong.

It loves parties and entertainment, and is anything but shy. It is capable of acting without hesitation. It demonstrates facility in gaining and holding the attention of others.

This segment loves power and can become very depressed if it becomes sick or feels tired. Often it will display a talent for making money. It responds strongly to praise and adoration, and wants to return love given it. It feels a great obligation to itself and will cultivate its talents with loving care. It makes an excellent parent, and wants to be proud of its children.

In more refined typed, the energy will manifest in a subtler manner, making them more quiet but with a definite charisma.

The Tarot: Leo (The Sun, #19) combines with Leo (The Sun, #19) to produce Neptune (The Enchantress, #11). Hence, happiness which is pure and unmixed with other emotional feelings is a great source of strength and spiritual power.

Leo 5°-7½° *Virgo:*

The individuality attempts to refine itself in this segment. The empty bombast which is usually associated with the undeveloped Leo is not to be found here. This segment desires the right to the crown as well as the crown itself. Its greatest need is to feel worthy and to purify itself.

It is concerned with what others think and wants to have a clean record. It is difficult for this segment to go against the dictates of society. Much moral conflict can exist here due to a compelling urge to do what is right, on the one hand, and to protect of established tradition on the other. It approaches social change well within the bounds of the law, and will present persuasive arguments for its case.

This segment needs to succeed. It sets up standards for itself and then tries to attain to them. It knows how to make itself happy, therefore can obtain contentment by direct approach. It loves to be busy and will often seek out a professional career. (This segment would be typical for doctors).

It has an eager desire to improve itself through a deeper and increasingly detailed and vivid understanding of its inner qualities. We might label this segment, "Precision in self-expression."

The Tarot: Leo (The Sun #19), combines with Virgo (Veiled Isis, #2) to produce the Sun (The Adept, #21). Hence, the self desires to be purified so that it may reflect divine light. This desire eventually is fulfilled because it is in line with the force of evolution.

Leo 7½°-10° *Libra:*

The nature of this segment is refined. It presents an amiable exterior. It enjoys activity and meeting others, socially and thru work. It is inspired by life. It likes a position of power and command and when it attains this it makes judicious decisions. It is tactful, and gets things done. It treats others as its equal and wants the same treatment in return. This segment has strong socio-political connotations, and people who have it emphasized in their charts are likely to be outgoing and involved in groups.

It may show an intense dislike of open conflict. It wants harmony among people. It dislikes conflict within itself.

Its nature is agreeable and compromising, yet it will eventually do what it wants, even if its actions produce hostility in others. It will not be overrun by others which might obstruct its plans.

It is loved for being able to say the right thing at the right time and for having social aplomb. It must beware of attempting to get what it wants through falsity.

The Tarot: Leo (The Sun, #19) combines with Libra (Isis Unveiled, #3) to produce Pluto (The Materialist,

94

#22). Hence, inspiration manifests in action which leads to the attainment of spiritual power. The individual reaches a balance of his inner nature that makes it possible for him to transcend.

Leo 10°-12½° *Scorpio:*

This is the most high-minded and exalted segment of Leo. It conceives of reality in abstract terms. Its primary conflict is between its higher and lower self. It feels a responsibility to live up to its potential ideal self image.

It wants to be independent and capable of singlehandedly overcoming difficulties. It never sees itself as being limited. Unaffected by failure, it is willing to try again. It loves learning and experience — it will go anywhere new or do anything different. It is often interested in religion, law, or occultism.

Its mentality is healthy and seeks out what is beneficial for its mantainance and development.

Negatively, it must beware of delusions of grandeur, and the over-spending of its energies. It can wear itself out by attempting to go in many directions at once. It needs to develop a sense of completion and stick to an endeavor long enough to learn from it.

It is full of good ideas, but needs to pick certain ones which can be developed to fruition.

The Tarot: Leo (The Sun, #19) combines with Scorpio (The Sovereign, #4) to produce Jupiter (The Hierophant, #5). Hence, the individual comes to the realization of his goal and this realization causes expansion of the conscious mind.

Leo 12½°-15° *Sagittarius:*

Leo symbolizes the formation of the individual man. In this segment this process is expansive. It tends to move away from the petty to the universal. This segment's sense of personal worth is assured, because it will reject limitations. It can admit errors. The irony of the situation is its pride in its humbleness. Its sense of its potential is acute, to the point that it must beware of feeling degraded by its present state of imperfection.

It can show happiness in the dreariest of situations. Its makeup is capable of bearing much weight due to its simplicity of philosophy.

It strives to control the natural forces which surround it without fighting them on their own level.

It definitely attempts to look at the bright side. Chronic depression will be rarely if ever found here. Any step in the right direction is considered a major accomplishment; no victory over the self is minor.

Negatively, it should beware of stubbornness because this trait can manifest with surprising force. The challenge of this segment: transcendence of the earthly ego.

The Tarot: Leo (The Sun, #19) combines with Sagittarius (The Conquerer, #7) to produce Capricorn (The Balance, #8). Hence, happiness which is able to transcend material concerns can dominate matter and therefore stabilize the imbalance between body and spirit.

Leo 15°-17½° *Capricorn:*

This segment displays a desire to live by a definite set of rules. It is the individual at his most rigid. The karma here will be the testing of faith and endurance. This segment feels that it knows what is right and wants to live this knowledge. The mind will ususally be concerned with moral crises which can seem unintelligible or unnecessary to others.

This segment is very set in its ways, and it is through this crystallization of character that it can learn about itself. It does not believe in a personal moral code. Instead, it sees its knowledge of truth as something which must be communicated to others so they can accept it. It does not believe in the precept, "live and let live." Its inspiration tells it that all must act within identical boundaries of cosmic order. It can be easily intimidated by organized religion. Therefore it must learn to accept eternal forgiveness taught by Christ.

It listens closely and carefully to people. It is anxious to hear other ideas so that it may compare them with its own. Others may say that it takes itself too seriously. It is capable of overblowing an issue "as a matter of principle." Its critical faculties are in constant operation. If it can hold its straight and narrow course long enough, it will succeed.

It has the ability to express itself with an economy of means.

The Tarot: Leo (The Sun, #19) combines with Capricorn (The Balance, #8) to produce Aquarius (The Sage, #9). Hence the volatile fire of individuality becomes crystallized into wisdom.

Leo 17½°-20° *Aquarius:*

This segment is the wise man who is liberated rather than hemmed in by what he knows. It makes free and creative use of the ideas it encounters. Its

Leonine fixity is less rigid than is commonly found in the fixed signs. It considers the possibility that the codes by which it lives are not pure enough to fit the situations it encounters. Therefore it is willing to experiment and take exceptions to rules to see what will happen. By this means it revises knowledge and re-evaluates its morality. It is experimental yet controlled and careful in its self-testing.

It likes the unique, so is full of surprises. It appreciates unexpected happenings as an opportunity to penetrate deeper into the meaning of reality.

There is self-betrayal here which is similiar in influence to what some astrologers ascribe to the Moon's South Node. It can be used as a positive asset though — a tool of learning so that this segment can get a better picture of how it is functioning by going against its normal mechanical motions.

It sees itself in other people and often attempts to emulate those whom it respects. It likes direct involvement in life and will often be attracted to games of sports.

It likes occupations in which there is much variety, rather than jobs which have set routines. It can manifest calm in crisis situations.

This segment rules experimental theater.

The Tarot: Leo (The Sun, #19) combines with Aquarius (The Sage, #9) to produce Uranus (The Wheel, #10). Hence, inspiration is the resource which feeds wisdom and vitalizes truths so that they may be applied to life.

Leo 20°-22½° *Pisces:*

This is the segment of self-dedication and self-worship. It is the poet. It works out stress (karma) through inspired creation. Its works have a powerfully cathartic quality. It loves to communicate and sees the reality around it as talking back to it in an everchanging symbolism. It will take good care of itself and its children, and is a dedicated parent.

The structure of personality is loose and open to a variety of influences. This segment yearns for inner discovery and likes to live intensely. The self-confidence is well-developed.

It tries to be reliable and responsible.

It is concerned with improving itself and will try things that contribute to its health, mental or physical.

Its romantic life is often fraught with difficulty, due to its lack of compromise. It wants to get along with others without giving in to them. It can be spontaneously generous, but will not betray its own makeup to secure the comfort of someone else. It requires relationships which are intimate yet as free as possible. It wants a give and take which is mutual without having to play the role of subject or object.

It has to realize that its burdens are self-made not fated, and can be rejected at will. It is easy for this segment to become enamored of old ways and habits.

Negatively it may be "hung up" in its self-image.

The Tarot: Leo (The Sun, #19) combines with Pisces (The Martyr, #12) to produce Scorpio (The Sovereign, #4). Hence, the self is dedicated to its own deepest needs, and, in its attempts to fulfill them achieves realization.

Leo 22½°-25° *Aries:*

This is Leo's most dramatic segment. It acts as if it were on stage. It is highly self-expressive. It sees itself going through great and far-reaching changes. As long as it can sustain this myth of self-renewal it can function effectively. It often has interest in religion and mysticism, especially the exotic or sublime. It may even develop a saint-complex. It accepts its creed in a deeply personal manner.

This segment's Jupiterian nature tries to emulate the Sun. It wants to transcend being a mere planet. (Jupiter's twelve moons, the largest number of satellites belonging to any planet in this solar system, make it a mirror of the solar system.) This segment may rebel against authority (Sun) and/or set itself up as an authority in its own right and attract pupils (moons). Its motives are high, but its "Jovial" nature may cause it to take responsibility too lightly. It is in danger of transforming itself through delusions of grandeur, rather than accomplishing something sound enough to stand on. It needs to *become* a Guru before it sets itself up as one.

Its deception is the most insidious kind: inadvertant. Positively, it can render dazzling and charismatic performances.

The Tarot: Leo (The Sun, #19) combines with Aries (The Reaper, #13) to produce Jupiter (The Hierophant, #5). Hence, the self is resiliant enough to withstand its own transformations and through this, grows in stature. True inspiriation will have a definite effect wherever it flowers.

Leo 25°-27½° *Taurus:*

This segment is attractive because it knows how to be natural. Its mannerisms are striking because they are so direct. It has a well-developed sense of style. Negatively, it must beware of clinging too closely to itself as it is — falling in love with its own imperfections.

This segment is in touch with the roots of its being. It has vivid memories of childhood and feels protective of its family background. It's proud of its heritage.

It is able to do the best with what it has and to be satisfied. This can be a deficit though, because it will subvert the natural desire to want more, which leads to evolution. It must strive to change and experiment so that its existence will not become stale. It needs to accept the fact that there may be a gap between what it thinks it is and what it really is. It needs to suspend its natural urge to judge itself and others before it has really looked at what it is judging. Strength of character is here and all it needs to be meaningful is spiritual fiber. The instinct to protect the ego has been well-developed. Now the requirement is to relax these defenses at the proper time.

This segment signifies "solidity of self-image."

The Tarot: Leo (The Sun, #19) combines with Taurus (The Alchemist, #14) to produce Venus (The Two Paths, #6). Hence, the individual is capable of self-regeneration, and must be careful to avoid the temptation of perpetuating his faults and shortcomings. The love of Divine Self must transcend the love of self.

Leo 27½°-30° *Gemini:*

The individual here is intent on finding happiness. This segment is aware of polar opposites within itself and can experience much interior struggle. The ego may go through many erratic changes feeling alternately inferior and superior.

101

Much self-searching takes place here, but there is unshakeable confidence that the right things will eventually be discovered. It is aware of itself as being imcomplete and in a state of formation. Natural wisdom is here because this segment knows how to be both self-assertive and tentative. It realizes that self-assertion needs inner humbleness to be effective, and that being tentative need never be an embarrassment to the ego. It sense its dual nature of being both debased man (Adam after the Fall) and God Incarnate (Bodhisattva).

It may feel it has failed, but it will rarely feel that it cannot succeed if it tries. It always has energy, and when it thinks it has reached its limits, it will usually find that its limits have been expanded.

It wants to be wise, and to experience everything that it can. It wants to know itself and it realizes that the only way to accomplish this is to know the not-self as well. Its being is tempered through action.

Self-assurance will only come to this segment if its self-image is *clear*.

The Tarot: Leo (The Sun, #19) combines with Gemini (The Star, #17) to produce Aquarius (The Sage, #9). Hence, the individual, in realizing his dual nature, acquires the hope and faith to achieve wisdom.

Virgo 0°-2½° *Gemini:*

This segment symbolizes the birth of the desire for perfection. It desires purity which is complete on all levels. The mind is practical and idealistic. It wants to see its ideals incarnated in material form. It can be nervous and hurried. It tends to rush around a problem, attacking it now from this angle and now from that. Great frustration is often the result. It can see the pot of gold at the end of the rainbow but may not know how to reach it.

Its clairvoyant potential is high. Its critical faculty concentrates on the loop holes in logic and through these may escape to a higher realm. This segment has the makings of a fine psychologist. It can discern truth on multiple levels, and has a sharp instinct for discerning falsity, although it may not be able to prove the knowledge it receives from the inner plane.

It is quite perceptive about itself, sometimes painfully so. Claustrophobia, or a fear of being cornered is sometimes indicated.

This segment is happiest when it educates its conscious mind as a counterbalancing of its psychic faculty. This helps it deal more effectively with the subjective half of its insight.

The Tarot: Virgo (Veiled Isis, #2) combines with Gemini (The Star, #17) to produce Leo (The Sun, #19). Hence, cognizance of the unseen world gives hope in discerning the truth of the existence of the absolute. If this is accomplished, the individual eventually becomes a Sun — a realized source of radiant spiritual energy.

Virgo 2½°-5° *Cancer:*

Virgo's purity is willing to test itself by submitting to temptation. This segment can be in close contact with the spirit world — the plane where both angels and ghosts exist. It does not see its goodness as something to be protected, but rather as a quality which can be subjected to evil and still exist unchanged. It dares to battle the devil.

I have refrained from drawing examples from famous people to point up certain aspects of these segments, but I feel an example displays the force of this segment most effectively: Helena Blavatsky, whom the astrologer Marc Jones has called the greatest occultist of the Twentieth Century, has her Mars and Saturn here. She was known to have communicated with many spirits, both high and low.

In those people who would shy away from an open exchange with those on the astral level, this segment will still cause them to be prompted by discarnates, whether they know it or not. The parapsychological ability is often striking.

This segment can be secretive. Its karma concerns being deceived by its own concept of what is positive. It may come to a shocking awareness that the demon with which it is tangling is none other than itself. This realization can, if handled with right action, trigger liberation. A crisis of consciousness can lead to an awareness of the immortality of the God within.

The Tarot: Virgo (Veiled Isis, #2) combines with Cancer (The Moon, #18) to produce the Moon (The Sarcophagus, #20). Hence, knowledge of the absolute makes it possible to deal with the deceptions perpetrated on the astral plane. This can lead to a reawakening of dead hopes and eventual fulfillment.

Virgo 5°-7½° *Leo*
This segment is aware of its short-comings, but its attitude toward them is healthy. It attempts to overcome its limitations rather than to judge itself. If it fails it is inspired to try again. It knows that there can be no giving up, not even in death. Others will see it as

being severely self-critical. Of all the segments of Virgo, it has the most potent spirit of perfection.

It knows that its conscious mind is incomplete, and it pushes itself to see the hidden self.

It develops its own way of doing things. Trying to emulate someone else's manner can be difficult for this segment.

Extremely self-willed, this segment is not easily influenced by other people. It thinks things through and makes up its mind for itself. It believes that something is not worth doing unless it is done right. Its romantic involvements may fail due to its well-developed sense of independence. It can co-exist with someone and not care to penetrate that person's mind or plumb his depths. If the relationship works, it feels that there is no reason to analyze it. If it doesn't, it is likely to go on to something else. It cannot be overly concerned with someone else. Its karma is to keep its mind on the business of its own being.

It can be dangerous for this segment to "fall in love," since the stress release from the libido can overshadow the personality to the extent that more fulfilling goals are, for the time being, forgotten.

The Tarot: Virgo (Veiled Isis, #2) combines with Leo (The Sun, #19) to produce the Sun (The Adept, #21). Hence, purity becomes a source of inspiration which can flood the whole being with divinity.

Virgo 7½°-10° *Virgo:*

This segment is diligent. It does things carefully and thoroughly. Its critical faculty is well-developed, but it will rely on its intuition in the final analysis. Reason here is a tool — and only a tool. This segment

105

might have trouble finishing projects because it keeps redoing to "get all the bugs out."

It segment operates like a twelfth house influence, but in its positive as well as its traditionally negative interpretation. The twelfth house is the hidden supports as well as the hidden handicaps, and one can be used to subvert the other. The self's deepest failings are recognized as well as those good qualities which are better developed than average.

This segment is preoccupied with the various ways in which things can be known. It tends to accept information in terms of its source, rather than debating the correctness of the information itself. It weighs the pros and cons of a situation. It is agreeable and open to new ideas or new approaches to things.

The mind is sharp and clear. It thinks in neat patterns and likes to plan and outline. Its concentration on details can eventually lead to a revising of its world view. It believes that truth has to be applicable at all times and places.

The Tarot: Virgo (Veiled Isis, #2) combines with Virgo (Veiled Isis, #2) to produce Scorpio (The Sovereign, #4). Hence, true science is a combination of objective and subjective knowledge. To study it in its completeness brings self-realization.

Virgo 10°-12½° *Libra:*

This is the segment of the applied scientist. It wants to make practical use of abstractions in the world of matter. It is interested in details, as is typical of Virgo, but it will not let details stop it from acting. It is more aggressive than Virgo is usually thought to be. It operates effectively in the role of executor — one who

106

carries out the plans made by others and who takes care of the details.

It must beware of taking on too much. It tries to concentrate on both major problems and minor details at the same time and so doing could possibly give an inferiority complex, since it is so concerned with responsibility.

It likes to work in partnership with others and does not mind playing a secondary role. It is good at taking orders. Its manner is feminine and industrious.

This segment will live by what it believes, although is not a rebel. The fighting spirit is not here, but rather a quiet manner of going one's own way. This segment will not involve itself in disputes unless something blocks its way or corners it.

It usually does not stop learning. It loves studying, schools, books, and anything else which it feels will be uplifting. Its mind seeks exercise.

More than anything, it wants to see the fruits of its labor.

The Tarot: Virgo (Veiled Isis, #2) combines with Libra (Isis Unveiled, #3) to produce Jupiter (The Hierophant, #5). Hence, science which is actively applied in the outside world is the true religion. Action based on purity causes expansion.

Virgo 12½°-15° *Scorpio:*

This is a segment which likes research. It is inquisitive. It has respect for science, especially in its non-uniform and infinite aspect. It is intrigued by the oddities of nature — the non-conformities and curiosities. The mind is sharp and enjoys working out puzzles. Its reasoning is empirical — it starts with what it sees as a particular case and from there works toward general principles. It is fascinated by secrets.

It is a good critic and advisor, and will usually show much expertise in its own field. It is capable of penetrating and insightful analysis.

It may develop a fetish of cleanliness, typified by Freud's anal-neurotic syndrome. A love of purity and precision can develop into an abhorrance of dirt stemming from a repression of sexual feelings. A parent whose child has this segment emphasized should be careful to avoid any negative conditioning concerning toilet training, or overstressing cleanliness.

Positively, this segment is meant to find faults which are difficult to pinpoint and to offer solutions for them. It is good at work which requires a high level of excellence. In the arts, its technical ability can be amazing. It is capable of creating an aura of purity around whatever it does.

The Tarot: Virgo (Veiled Isis, #2) combines with Scorpio (The Sovereign, #4) to produce Venus (The Two Paths, #6). Hence, the hidden secrets of nature, when realized and brought to light, must be used to further evolution. Correct use of scientific knowledge is the test here.

Virgo 15°-17½° *Sagittarius:*

This segment seeks out tasks which seem impossible. Rather than seeing perfection as contained in a final product, it seeks perfection in the ongoing process. This process is limited by this segment's state of mind and the limitations on its working conditions. When perfection has been reached, this segment goes on to something bigger, better, and more difficult, thus competing with itself.

Much nervous energy is present. Everything is approached with objectivity and planning. If circumstances cause the plans to fail, more plans are made. This segment tends to collect information in a compulsive manner. It wants the news. It is usually concerned about health and interested in diet and nutrition. It wants to keep pace with everything at once and can exhaust itself.

The intellectual function may be overdeveloped to the point that it causes rather than solves problems. This segment has to learn when and how to shut itself off. This will help to allow its intuitive faculties to operate more freely.

It is quite apt to get hung up in details, moreso than any other segment of Virgo. Tension can build when it can't fulfill potential due to circumstances. It yearns for transcendent perfection.

The Tarot: Virgo (Veiled Isis, #2) combines with Sagittarius (The Conquerer, #7) to produce Aquarius (The Sage, #9). Hence, hidden knowledge, when used by the spirit to attain victory over matter will be supportive of true wisdom.

Virgo 17½°-20° *Capricorn:*

This segment seeks a clear and definite set of ideals which it can put into practice freely and creatively. It is erratically changeable in its personal relationships because it attempts to bring about internal attitudes which will balance its emotions with its circumstances.

It likes things which are simple and wants a system of thought which in no way contradicts itself. It may tend to cling too closely to its own personal bias.

Positively, it senses how far it can go and therefore will rarely overestimate its capacity. It tends to retreat from situations which are upsetting. It refuses to be cornered in a meaningless role and throws off its bonds forcefully and suddenly.

It is a protector of innocence — its own or anybody's. It will defend pure ideas against those who would try to twist or cloud them. It is loyal to its cause if a worthy one.

The temperment is alternately easy-going and rigid, depending on whether if feels secure or challenged. Many ups and downs in partnerships are indicated.

The Tarot: Virgo (Veiled Isis, #2) combines with Capricorn (The Balance, #8) to produce Uranus (The Wheel, #10). Hence, hidden knowledge, when used with justice can reverse the workings of fate and release the individual from the wheel of karma.

Virgo 20°-22½° *Aquarius:*

This segment has a sensitive and touchy physical makeup and needs to watch its diet. Mental and emotional problems can result from the wrong foods.

This segment is critical of itself without being harsh. It will work to rid itself of a fault without regret for having it. Its approach to life is more direct and less timid than is usually thought of Virgo. It wants to be itself and follow its own inner voice without hesitating or feeling guilty. This segment wants to make its own decisions. It is not swayed by the advice of others. It listens and decides for itself. It would rather not be confused by the criticisms of others.

It can develop great inner power if it can find time and solitude to do so. It is easily overshadowed by other people and needs to stay away from those who would try to dominate.

The need to act out what is inside the self is nearly

compulsive. This segment will stay under no one's thumb for long. It knows that it can be completely self-sufficient, and this is what it strives for.

Unfulfilled desires are very frustrating. It needs free reign in its work, rather than a situation where it has no say-so. Above all it desires to maintain a sense of loyalty to its responsibilities.

The Tarot: Virgo (Veiled Isis, #2) combines with Aquarius (The Sage, #9) to produce Neptune (The Enchantress, #11). Hence, science, when coupled with wisdom generated by experience produces great force and spiritual power.

Virgo 22½°-25° *Pisces:*

Industry is the keynote of this segment. Here the naturally busy Virgo takes on the dedication of Pisces. It feels a duty toward refining itself and its potentials. The life's work is held in highest esteem, and the rest of the being revolves around this single factor.

The respect for knowledge is great.

This segment likes to work behind the scenes. It is happiest when it has ample time to devote to its private life. It regenerates itself by going on retreats. It works best alone rather than in partnership. It wants to be left to itself to do what it has to do.

It is amazingly resourceful and can rise above handicaps through devoting its attention to it. It is powerfully motivated to cure itself of its problems, whether these be physical, financial, social, or any other. It will take care of its own problems before dealing with those of others. It may be accused of being selfish.

It believes that "an ounce of prevention is worth a pound of cure," and so would rather look for its trouble before trouble looks for it.

111

It must avoid becoming completely entangled in details.

The Tarot: Virgo (Veiled Isis, #2) combines with Pisces (The Martyr, #12) to produce Taurus (The Alchemist, #14). Hence, when the self is devoted to the science of being, regeneration is the result.

Virgo 25°-27½° Aries:

This segment is very self-concerned. It tends to have few close friends. The Virgoan urge to analyze and perfect is directed inward. It may want to isolate itself as much as possible from outside influences. It is usually set in its ways and does not want to have to deal with the opinions of others. At worst it can be a slave to tradition.

It takes its work personally. Creativity is an outlet for its deep emotions and stresses. It feels happy and secure when laboring, because this obliterates its sense of isolation and lonliness. If its problems are great, it may devote so much time to a career that social life is excluded.

It will experience many personality changes throughout its life. This is due to sudden realizations which tend to upset its internal structure. It is strong enough to endure these periods because the roots of its being are sturdy.

Virgo here uses Arian fire to effect its purification. The external appearance of this segment may be morose and depressive, but deep within the self is an optimism and hopefulness. This positive spark is strong but may not manifest on the surface.

This segment tends to love challenging responsibilities.

The Tarot: Virgo (Veiled Isis, #2) combines with

112

Aries (The Reaper, #13) to produce Saturn (The Black Magician, #15). Hence, when the laws of secret science are used to effect a transformation of being, whatever is predestined will become purified. Fate awaits oneself in the future, but the actions of the present are constantly changing its nature.

Virgo 27½°-30° *Taurus:*

This segment experiences transmutations of character which come from deep within, and which can occur abruptly. The mind is usually set in its beliefs, and the personality is capable of bearing up under great strain. The self-protection instinct is strong.

This segment is powerful and aggressive. It is usually intent on purifying and refining things which already exist. It leans toward conservatism and a respect of traditional values.

It is a perfectionist and will stick to a job until it is complete. It has animal vitality in abundance and its primary goal is to find the means to harness this power so that it can be used to its greatest benefit. It is sensual without being languorous. The energies operate carefully, and without faltering. It holds itself in close check so that the blind force contained inside it can be released slowly and steadily through the valve of its discipline.

It is adept at knowing how to simplify. It can remove the frills from an idea until only the major components are left, and divested of their adornments, these take on a new vigor.

The Tarot: Virgo (Veiled Isis, #2) combines with Taurus (The Alchemist, #14) to produce Mars (The Lightning, #16). Hence, the secrets of nature, revealed by science and used to rejuvenate positive and benign forces, will naturally destroy what is negative and no longer of use. Destroying ignorance first leaves man with nothing, but giving knowledge first forces ignorance out as a matter of course.

Libra 0°-2½° *Taurus:*

Libra is the sign of movement, activity, relationship and productivity. Its first dwadashamsa is subruled by Taurus, showing that the initial purpose of fruitfulness is to maintain a proper balance of the combination of forces in reality. This segment attempts to keep things on an even keel, strengthening the weakest link in the chain. Any kind of labor has a therapeutic effect on it. When it feels that it is accomplishing something, it is positively reinforced. It has fine stamina due to an innate knowledge of how to pace itself. It is intent on perfecting whatever it does.

It approaches a job by feeling out what it has to do. It may be awkward when it is unfamiliar with the tools, ideas, and methods it is using, but when familiarity has been gained, it can perform its task in an intuitive manner. It enjoys routines, and operates most effectively when patterns remain constant.

This segment's greatest problem is bridging the gap between conscious objectivity and automatic uncontrollable responses. It needs to work toward definite goals rather than becoming sidetracked by other issues. Self-discipline is the answer.

The Tarot: Libra (Isis Unveiled, #3) combines with Taurus (The Alchemist, #14) to produce Gemini (The Star, #17). Hence, action which is perpetually main-

114

tained is the basis of hope. Change is constant — this is the immortal law of the cosmos.

Libra 2½°-5° *Gemini:*

This segment is highly versatile. It is aggressive and yet agreeable. It likes to have more than one project going at once and can always find something with which to occupy itself. At worst, its movements may be nothing more than nervous habits. It loves *doing,* more than *starting* and *finishing*. It may drop a project for years, but if given enough time, it will return to it.

Inner conflicts are solved swiftly and on an emotional basis. It wants to be able to see all sides of a thing at once, but on the other hand, it would rather act immediately even it if is not fully aware of what it is doing.

It tends to ingest ideas and then digest them. Anything new encountered is mulled over in the mind. This segment tries to decide how it feels and a decision is usually followed by abundant activity based on the new idea.

This segment has a talent for seeing its own opportunities. It loves to do things with other people. It needs a marriage partner who has a wide range of interests. It is capable of great faith and trust in its friends and relates to others in a lively manner.

The Tarot: Libra (Isis Unveiled, #3) combines with Gemini (The Star, #17) to produce the Moon (The Sarcophagus, #20). Hence, activity with hope and faith as its basis can bring new life to a lost cause.

Libra 5°-7½° *Cancer:*

This segment is Libra at its most productive. Like a mother its foremost concern is the birth of its child. It labors to fulfill its desire to bring its creation to culmination. Its actions are definite and direct. Activity (Libra) becomes a medium for the soul, and by acquiring what it wants most, this segment may learn more about itself. The way to see the true nature of a desire is to satisfy it. Otherwise, the desire will continue to exist and cause stress.

It must be careful to avoid devoting energies to the attainment of negative goals, such as revenge. However, even if it does this, all will turn out well because wrong desire completely fulfilled brings realization of the misdirected energy. The audacity here knows no bounds and therefore can be destructive. On the other hand, the first rule of life is adhered to: body and spirit combine for the purpose of action, and it is through trial and error that truth is discovered.

This is illustrated in the character of Macbeth in the extreme: Macbeth achieves tragic status by completely embracing his own damnation — and having the courage of that commitment.

The Tarot: Libra (Isis Unveiled, #3) combines with Cancer (The Moon, #18) to produce the Sun (The Adept, #21). Hence, to be fruitful, activity must continue to brave the unknown, (the valley of the shadow of death), and in this manner human life will be fulfilled.

Libra 7½°-10° *Leo*

This segment is a powerful diplomat. The inspirational nature of Leo adds tact and smoothness to the actions. This segment relies on its personality to carry it through situations, and it attains positions of power because it can make itself well-liked with little effort. It is good at bluffing its way.

116

It prides itself on being an individual. It has all the outer trappings of a leader, but needs to make this felt within as well.

It does not appear dominating and this very thing makes domination easy for it to indulge in.

It wants to do things its own way and this can lead to true originality or an attempt to find new methods when the old ones were adequate. Things are executed with a personal touch.

Its creativity tends to manifest in everything it does rather than in a limited field of endeavor. Although it likes teamwork it would rather work alone than to answer to a critical partner for its actions.

The Tarot: Libra (Isis Unveiled, #3) combines with Leo (The Sun, #19) to produce Pluto (The Materialist, #22). Hence, activity which is self-inspiring can be either a source of spiritual power or blind foolishness.

Libra 10°-12½° *Virgo:*

The active Libra wants to base its actions on precise methods. This segment wants do the most effective thing possible at every moment of its existence. It is a planner. It wants to solve its problems with a minimum of effort. It fears involvement in insignificant or meaningless activity. It needs to have a subjective feeling of importance and this is its prime motivation.

Negatively it can be too perfectionistic. It acts compulsively and will toil away at something as long as there is a flaw to be seen or imagined.

This segment most desires harmonious activity. It is good at relegating jobs. In teamwork it will take the less desirable tasks and would rather see things accomplished than debated. It likes to be busy.

It senses that its existence is for some definite purpose. Therefore it cannot become involved in things for which it has personal feeling. Conversely, it will bring a uniqueness of self to its endeavors.

The Tarot: Libra (Isis Unveiled, #3) combines with Virgo (Veiled Isis, #2) to produce Jupiter (The Heirophant, #5). Hence, the activity which works out karma is successful and expansive.

Libra 12½°-15° *Libra:*

This segment's best quality is decisiveness. Its movements are flowing. It drifts with the general current of affairs and takes part in the activity going on around it. It joins in without being overly aggressive or passive. This is the segment of sheer undifferentiated movement.

It takes the path of least resistance. It believes that the means justify the ends, and so can misrepresent its true feelings just to get what it wants. It needs to promote sincere harmony.

It can be artfully tactful and pleasant. It is social in its orientation and wants to be accepted and loved by everyone.

Its greatest difficulty is an inability to make up its mind. It is easily tempted to go against its own resolutions. It has difficulty effecting self-discipline.

Upsets can appear here that seemingly come from nowhere. This happens because of an inborn trait of putting off distasteful tasks or repressing hostilities.

The Tarot: Libra (Isis Unveiled, #3) combines with Libra (Isis Unveiled, #3) to produce Venus (The Two Paths, #6). Hence, activity which is grooved in its own

118

mode of being will eventually wear out its groove and change pattern. This, in the final analysis, is good.

Libra 15°-17½° *Scorpio:*

The most agressive qualities of Libra are manifested here. The attention is one-pointed because the mind looks to eliminate inconsequentials. The ideals are usually simple and upheld stubbornly. This segment tries to practice what it preaches. It is concerned with philosophical problems only as far as they are related to its immediate life. It has no use for the posing of questions which have no bearing on the here and now. It must have a completely sound reason for acting and if it cannot see a clear-cut purpose it will not get involved.

It is success-oriented and needs a clearly defined goal. It will put no energy in travelling toward some cloudy destination. It wants a cause, but the cause must be palpable. It desires sound working methods for greatest proficiency.

It wants to know the reasons for every step it takes and will argue over proceedures until it understands the entire project. If it decides that the course of action is wrong, choose another.

It wants to be in command when it relates to others.

The Tarot: Libra (Isis Unveiled, #3) combines with Scorpio (The Sovereign, #4) to produce Sagittarius (The Conquerer, #7). Hence, activity which is not blind, but based on a knowledge of the true nature of reality, can rise above material concerns and be uninhibited by physical law.

Libra 17½°-20° *Sagittarus:*

This segment is one which achieves success through outwitting its opponent. The nature is subtly combative. It is good at solving puzzles or problems because it is versed in the arts of logic and surprise attack. It is active, and does not rely much on plans. It likes to do several related things at once and needs variety.

It tends to work in bursts of energy and can experience sudden explosions of creative inspiration. Sometimes it will resolve a difficulty seemingly by accident. Its intuition is eccentric.

Its best asset is the ability to know when it has made a mistake. Its work may, at worst, be slipshod, but at best shows an easy and relaxed vitality.

It can get itself both into and out of difficulty with great speed. It is adept at improvisation, but should beware of thoughtless activity.

It has ambivalent feelings about tradition. On one hand it senses the worth inherent in accepted social values, but on the other it desires to do away with customs or established notions which it feels are useless. Because of this, its behavior can be irregular and show many idiosyncrasies. This segment's need and desire: to transcend the earthly problems of relating.

The Tarot: Libra (Isis Unveiled, #3) combines with Sagittarius (The Conquerer, #7), to produce Uranus (The Wheel, #10). Hence, for activity to achieve victory, it must be capable of suddenly shifting its course. All games (and battles) are governed by the same rule: expect and be prepared for the unexpected.

Libra 20°-22½° *Capricorn:*

This segment is silently aggressive. It generally has a strong constitution and can accomplish much work because of its steady approach.

A tendency to be self-righteous is indicated. This segment will fight for what it believes, but rather than let its morality inhibit the flow of accomplishment, it will compromise. It feels powerless when its activity is stopped because it wants to keep the ball rolling.

This segment needs routine. It operates best when it has learned the work that it is doing and is on familiar ground. Long projects are best because it is within the context of a large structure that it can exert its most potent influence.

This segment needs to search for what it can do best. It must beware of continuing a line of effort which has become empty. It needs to attack problems in a definite way and with a definite plan.

The Tarot: Libra (Isis Unveiled, #3) combines with Capricorn (The Balance, #8) to produce Neptune (The Enchantress, #11). Hence, action understood can transcent the law of cause and effect and solve problems at the unseen root level.

Libra 22½°-25° *Aquarius:*

This segment thirsts for experience and is ready to jump into the situation at hand. It wants to learn, not by taking in abstract information, but by doing field-work: the process of trial and error. It is productive and gains knowledge through studying its own productions.

It can be a devoted and active member of an organization or group.

It has a deep-rooted sense of responsibility. It feels best when it knows exactly what it is doing and so it will want to get all of the facts. It will want to learn everything possible about its own field.

It wants to occupy a position of importance and power.

It will go out of its way to help others, but it wants

121

complete acceptance of its methods in such help. It feels it cannot assist unless it is trusted.

The Tarot: Libra (Isis Unveiled, #3) combines with Aquarius (The Sage, #9) to produce Pisces (The Martyr, #12). Hence, action with wisdom as its basis will prefer to suffer now so it may be happy later. All fate has to be met and worked out, then the way is cleared to the Kindgom of Heaven.

Libra 25°-27½° *Pisces:*

It is necessary for this segment to live by routines, that is, to make its activities consistent, logical, and ordered. It can be compulsive in its manner of doing things. It likes to give to other people — to work for their happiness. It will be self-sacrificing, and can be devoted to a cause.

Negatively there can be selfishness here because of inflexibity. It has to serve in its own way and will give of itself on its own terms. It may not change itself or understand another's viewpoint.

In the arts, its creations will often manifest an elegant sense of form.

Its attractions to others can be obsessive. It feels that there are drives within itself which it does not dare repress. It must be true to itself. If it finds a person who will accept what it has to give and its mode of giving, it can be satisfied.

It is generally unselfish with material possessions and will give freely of the goods which it owns. It may be unable to do alone what it could do for someone else and this impulse of loving subjugation to others triggers productivity.

Needless to say, the breaking off of close bonds of

love can be devastating and it will go out of its way to prevent this. On the other hand, it may tend to feel "caught" in relationships.

The Tarot: Libra (Isis Unveiled, #3) combines with Pisces (The Martyr, #12) to produce Saturn (The Black Magician, #15). Hence, action which gives freely of the fruit of its endeavors is a positive sacrifice and in time, is destined to conquer limitations of personal fate.

Libra 27½°-30° *Aries:*

This segment tears down and rebuilds. It likes to watch transmutation and is not upset in the midst of chaos, because it knows that all storms subside. It can become bored when not exerting itself. It should beware of "jumping from the frying pan into the fire," because its urge to "jump" is perpetual. It is satisfied with things as they are for only brief moments.

It starts projects with a flurry of activity. Artisticly it sees itself as an aesthetic pioneer. Its manner of expression is self-assertive, but it avoids being blunt.

It often has problems finishing things, because its natural drive is toward the higher and it can lose interest in things begun on a lower level. It gets ahead of itself. It would rather leave things half-done than to complete something it no longer believes in. It wants its action to have definite value. It is aware of ever developing opportunities for expression.

It relates to situations in new ways.

The Tarot: Libra (Isis Unveiled, #3) combines with Aries (The Reaper, #13) to produce Mars (The Lightning, #16). Hence, action which is bold enough to transform will bring life closer to its divine goal by levelling obstacles which aren't strong enough to stand.

Scorpio 0°-2½° *Aries:*

This segment can be arbitrary. It tends to jump into situations on the spur of the moment. It likes to act, and will be able to perform whether or not it has rehearsed its part. It will be enlightened by its own reactions.

This is one of the most unpredictable segments of the zodiac. It makes plans but often deviates from them with no regrets. It is capable of dominating its own subconscious, but when its hidden self rebels against this dictatorship, it can reach a quick compromise. Its self-realization is ego-centric and fitful. No one can tell it about itself, but it may reach the same conclusion of its own accord.

It expresses pragmatically. It sees itself as a symbol of itself. Its manner is often blunt. It takes the attitude that the truth is best. When its cognizance of reality expands, its actions change accordingly. It trusts fate to bring what it needs and assumes that the experience is necessary to its development.

Consciousness here is an expression of universal mind — a part of the whole yet reflecting light in its own way. This segment's power is its freshness of awareness.

The Tarot: Scorpio, (The Soveriegn, #4) combines with Aries, (The Reaper, #13) to produce Gemini, (The Star, #17). Hence, realization causes trauma. When passed through, the experience leads to a more hopeful state.

Scorpio 2½°-5° *Taurus:*

This is the segment of the uncompromising individualist. It has personal vision which it fulfills in its own terms. It is fully autonomous.

There is much self-interest. This segment feeds upon and is nourished by itself. There is a dichotomy between its conscious and subconscious mind, with the conscious in a dominating position.

It wants to be true to itself. If distrubed it will turn inward to solve problems. Help from some outside source is usually no more than static to it. It is aware of its own infinite qualities and is unafraid of its unexplored depths. At times it may seem inconsistent to others, because it will not communicate its mental workings but rather makes some change at the end of a long thought process. It has the courage to be itself — no matter what level of development this may be.

It does not accept criticism because it feels it is doing the best it can. It might agree with advice that is given but must move at its own pace and will not allow outside forces to push it or slow it down.

The Tarot: Scorpio (The Sovereign, #4) combines with Taurus (The Alchemist, #14) to produce Cancer (The Moon, #18). Hence, personal realization which is regenerative and self-maintaining need not fear pitfalls. It is its own protector.

Scorpio 5°-7½° *Gemini*

Burning within the individual is the spark of the divine will. This segment is involved in finding this spark within itself.

It is forceful and aggressive. It is intent on doing

125

what it feels to be right and trusts its own decisions. Its will is firm.

A tremendous desire to succeed is here, but this segment will not betray its own ethics to get what it wants. If success is achieved, its because of courage in applying its talents. It is capable of waiting for what it wants, and adverse conditions tend to force it into being more persistent.

This segment desires much and works toward a variety of goals simultaneously. It likes to communicate and collect information from many sources. When in search of knowledge it will consult authorities.

There may be a tendency to confuse logic and feeling because this segment is bound up in its own notions. It realizes that anything can be rationalized, but it may not have the ability to do so.

The Tarot: Scorpio (The Sovereign, #4) combines with Gemini (The Star, #17) to produce the Sun (The Adept, #21). Hence, realization is inevitable, and when this is understood attainment can be patiently awaited.

Scorpio 7½°-10° *Cancer:*

This strongly sensuous nature is usually turned inward and manifests in fantasies. In love relationships this segment is very sensitive to the attitudes and reactions of the loved one.

Flashes of insight often come through dreams or through retreating within the self. This segment is not talkative and keeps most of its ideas inside. It is independent.

It is a natural medium and understands people intuitively.

It tends to get drawn into dangerous situations because it is fascinated with the unknown. It is loath to confide in others and when it does it is often betrayed.

It feels that it has to go its own way without outside interference.

It dwells just below the level of its conscious awareness and so can come up with unique insights. It enjoys reverie and may appear scatterbrained or absent-minded. It likes travel in both literal and figurative senses. It is typically happy late in life after weathering many experiences.

The Tarot: Scorpio (The Sovereign, #4) combines with Cancer (The Moon, #18) to produce Pluto (The Materialist, #22). Hence, the desire to become self-realized is strong. The unknown is bravely faced until force and spiritual power are developed.

Scorpio 10°-12½° *Leo:*

An exhuberant love of learning is expressed in this segment. Creativity is therapeutic for it. The self is thrown into the drives of the ego, so there is desire to compete with the self, and surpass present capabilities. This segment will listen to ideas that appeal to its higher nature. The self-image is usually healthy and well-developed.

This segment is uninhibited in the display of its personal oddities. It likes people who show it attention.

It likes open space and feeling in touch with the infinite. It is open to fresh ideas. It attempts to better itself without feeling embarrassed over past failures.

It wants deeply intimate relationships but is attracted to footloose and unpredictable types to save it from boredom. It usually plays the aggressive sexual role.

This segment likes to keep moving and to display its considerable talents and skills in actual performance.

The Tarot: Scorpio (The Sovereign, #4) combines with Leo (The Sun, #19) to produce Jupiter (The Heirophant, #5). Hence, joyously accepted realization is the truly religious attitude. The happiness of self-exploration creates the desire for more, until attainment is experienced.

Scorpio 12½°-15° *Virgo:*

A desire to understand, to question everything so the root-system as well as the branches of ideas are known. This segment has a genius for fault-finding. In love relationships it enjoys administering to others and is often quite submissive sexually.

It is mechanical-minded. Its approach to life is feminine, subtle, and indirect. Artisticly it tends to nurture its creations in the manner of a gardner, and its works develop slowly. It corrects itself, taking care of loose ends, so the end product will be clear. It is intrigued by the tools of its trade and does justice to the media with which it works. It has a genius for making fortunate decisions. At every step in its labors it is aware of divergent possibilities, and its choices are intuitive.

Is is adept at implication rather than the direct approach. It can subtly appeal to the emotions of another person without its methods being suspected.

The Tarot: Scorpio (The Soveriegn, #4) combines

128

with Virgo (Veiled Isis, #2) to produce Venus (The Two Paths, #6). Hence, the realizations which come from studying nature's secrets necessitate a choice in how one's knowledge will be used — as a source of illusion which retards development, or as a well-spring of power with which to uplift all life.

Scorpio 15°-17½° *Libra:*

Decisiveness sums up this segment in a word. Action based on knowledge is here in abundance. Also, there is a need to work and socialize with other people.

This segment often produces extreme attractiveness and a hidden refinement which is so subtle that it is difficult to describe.

Beauty is appreciated in terms of transformation. Awareness is felt as something which has to be acted upon. This segment is persistent in attempting to fulfill its own desires, even if it is not the best choice. It would rather try and fail than to have never tried at all.

It shies away from abstractions and wants to see potentials realized. Therefore it is not as interested in probability as in the result.

Patience is good for this segment. It should take a moment to think before going into action.

Scorpio's Martian aggression is in full flower here. It wants to get things done at all costs. This segment has the ability to handle situations smoothly.

The Tarot: Scorpio (The Sovereign, #4) combines with Libra, (Isis Unveiled, #3) to produce Sagittarius (The Conquerer, #7). Hence, realization is made manifest in activity, and action based on self-awareness cannot fail.

Scorpio 17½°-20° *Scorpio:*

This is the most strong-willed segment of Scorpio. It attempts to maintain its position in life and to be on top of circumstances. Its perception is acute, although possibly narrow.

This segment likes to lead a structured existence. It may be afraid of confusion to the point that it needs a place for everything and everything in its place. Others might say that it has a one-track mind. It needs to keep itself unclouded by side issues, and is therefore compelled to dispense with triviality to arrive at its goal. When it has made up its mind, nothing outside itself can change it.

Its means of sustaining its position, rather than pushing it forward, is highly feminine. It is a natural protector and can even be defiant.

It can be disdainful of anyone who does not understand it.

It wants to grasp its higher self and hold on forever. It searches for eternal ideas which will not change with time. It needs to maintain its balance apart from the rest of the world, and will rely on what has been tried and found to be true.

It manifests intensity of character and amazes others by its solidity. It may transcend the material.

The Tarot: Scorpio (The Sovereign,#4) combines with Scorpio (The Sovereign, #4) to produce Capricorn (The Balance, #8). Hence, pure realization is a matter of crystallization, and all matter, both organic and inorganic is a reflection of consciousness.

Scorpio 20°-22½° *Sagittarius:*

This segment attempts to find ideal applications for its ideas. It is a natural detective.

It is fascinated by simple and direct solutions to problems. It reworks the same ideas over and over, rather than trying new ones.

It may attempt a role in life before it is actually ready to play it. Its acting is highly believable.

It is resourceful in finding means to attain ends. It feels confident of handling any vicissitude successfully. It is independent.

It wants others to think that it has courage, so acts courageous even though it may feel quite timid.

It has a natural flair for sizing up situations in terms of what is truly happening rather than what appears on the surface.

It wants to make ideal use of what it has to offer, and therefore seeks to advance its knowledge in whatever field it calls its own. It never feels really confident, and so strives to expand its horizons and step up its personal powers.

The Tarot: Scorpio (The Sovereign, #4) combines with Sagittarius (The Conquerer, #7) to produce Neptune (The Enchantress, #11). Hence, realization, to manifest in victorious action, must function on subtler and subtler (and hence more powerful) levels.

Scorpio 22½°-25° *Capricorn:*

This segment can be strongly moralistic. It seeks to discipline itself so that it may maintain its higher nature even through periods of stress. It reminds itself

131

of truths to sustain pure motives. Its finest quality is a capacity for sustained effort even when it feels internal rebellion. It can receive sustained nourishment from a single exalted flash of what could be. It feels the urge to sacrifice itself for something and to defind its cause in an aggressive manner. This segment is sexually monogamous.

It must be able to work diligently for whatever it loves. It cannot admire from afar, because it needs to go out of its way to show its loyalty.

It may tend to dwell upon the past in a romantic dream-like manner: It mentally returns to its unforgettable experiences. Once in love, the flame may never completely die even after disasters and long periods of time.

All this segment need do is taste a purer form of happiness and it will stubbornly work to regain it. A promise of something better may keep it working for a lifetime.

The Tarot: Scorpio (The Sovereign, #4) combines with Capricorn (The Balance, #8) to produce Pisces (The Martyr, #12). Hence, realization which becomes fully developed is completely stable, and will lead the individual soul to self-sacrifice, as a means of working out karma.

Scorpio 25°-27½° *Aquarius:*

The highest good found here is a will which is transcendently uncompromising. If this segment sees a line of endeavor as being worthless, it will not tolerate it. It can become wise in a short time. It is inquisitive, but can be upset by being confronted with things for which it is not ready.

Many of this segment's realizations are initially

upsetting, but it will feel compelled to act on what it learns, even though it may shrink from what it feels it has to do.

It believes that anything that happens has the potential to make it wiser.

This segment can be painfully aware of how things should be, but can have problems applying this knowledge to its own reality. At worst this trait will manifest as frantic running from one absurdity to another in a fruitless waste of energy.

The Tarot: Scorpio (The Soverign, #4) combines with Aquarius (The Sage, #9) to produce Aries (The Reaper, #13). Hence realization tempered by the wisdom gained from experience will produce a break-up of stress and ultimately lead to liberation.

Scorpio 27½°-30° *Pisces:*

This segment is enigmatic and typically Scorpio. It is at once passive and feminine and yet forceful and aggressive. The evident quality is endurance. The nature is divinely stubborn. It will be moved by nothing outside itself. It cannot be out-waited because it is patient with a vengenance. Here is the masculine yang seed which is contained within the yin force.

Overbearing curiosity is here. This segment makes everything its business, because its overpowering ego sees everything as a reflection of its unexplored inner self. At worst it is subtly devious and can topple great edifices by tearing out a single carefully selected, stone.

It can be opinionated to the point of fanaticism and will go to any lengths to prove its intuitions. Its vision is purely personal and anything outside itself does not exist.

It sees that realization is more than just a chance thought which occurrs now and then. True realization has effect — it is a viable force which wells up like a volcano and purifies physical substance.

This segment needs to accept its inner drives and desires without feeling trapped by them.

The Tarot: Scorpio (The Soveriegn, #5) combines with Pisces (The Martyr, #12), to produce Mars (The Lightning, #16). Hence, realization which causes one to accept the lot in life and to serve the force of evolution faithfully, will finally strike down personal limitations.

Sagittarius 0°-2½° *Pisces:*

Perception, (Sagittarius), is initially based upon belief. (Pisces). The perception of higher realms, through refining the senses, is the meaning of this segment.

All that is percieved is valid. The perciever is the creator of what it experiences, and its creation is that on which it bases its beliefs. These beliefs operate as either hidden supports or hidden limitations.

This segment is wide open to any experience which may come its way. It is self-assertive in a very subtle manner. Its ego is unshakeable, so it has no desire to throw up protections around itself.

Beliefs are held to bridge gaps in knowledge. Once knowledge is obtained, then beliefs may be extended further. The development of the individuality may be seen as based on the interaction of seeing (knowing) and wanting to see (believing).

134

This segment signifies "surrender to the force of evolution."

The Tarot: Sagittarius (The Conquerer, #7) combines with Pisces (The Martyr, #12) to produce Leo (The Sun, #19). Hence, the victorious one must have dedication in order to achieve happiness. Using the will to conquer limits is the purpose. These limits cannot be conquered until they are reached.

Sagittarius 2½°-5° *Aries:*

Hope is the instrument of dominating matter through spirit. This segment realizes the newness of each moment. It revives itself by experiencing pure impulses from the subtlest levels of its being. It is intent on convincing others of truth as it recognizes it, and it wants more than just superficial agreement from others.

It is tranformed by its emotions and wants to give these emotions to others, so that they too will be transformed. It lives through reawakening to divine potential. Mind does in fact triumph over matter, but what this segment perceives is the fact that mind is always triumphing over matter. Esoterically, spirit is a state of being that knows no suffering. True success is not created, but exists inherent in all things. The universe was built to succeed.

This segment can feel permeated with inner happiness in the midst of outer tragedy because it is capable of seeing death as release rather than annihilation.

It knows that all is for one purpose — to be made perfect, and that seeming destruction only makes way for resurrection. Time is the mother of victory and all that happens within time contributes to victory's final birth.

This segment signifies the challenge of overcoming adversity.

The Tarot: Sagittarius (The Conquerer, #7) combines with Aries (The Reaper, #13) to produce the Moon (The Sarcophagus, #20). Hence, victory which transforms what it conquers will redeem what has been lost in the past and renew that which has become worn out.

Sagittarius 5°-7½° *Taurus:*

This segment attempts to slowly and steadily dominate its baser nature. It is aware of blind forces within itself and treats them with caution. It is always busy and its energy flow is persevering.

This is one of the more conservative segments of Sagittarius. Its purpose is to trimph over material concerns without destroying — to alter without defacing. It works with the materials at hand. It will try and try again, attempting one solution after another without becoming frustrated. It knows that every problem has a solution based on what is unique about that problem. This uniqueness is a manifestation of the "psychic imprint" of the situation and therefore holds the key to a possible cure or adjustment.

This segment tends to see flaws, or things to be made right, that other people would never categorize as such. It is never satisfied with a current level of perfection, but always wants to carry things to a higher and purer plane. It is intent on philosophical consistency.

The Tarot: Sagittarius (The Conquerer, #7) combines with Taurus (The Alchemist, #14) to produce the Sun (The Adept, #21). Hence, the victor who can keep his victory alive through its constant regeneration is truly a master.

Sagittarius 7½°-10° *Gemini:*

Optimism is found here in abundance. This segment is sure within itself that everything will work out. It has an uplifting influence on those around it.

It needs to learn how to stick to its goals. It has an easy manner of functioning and does not strain itself. It feels that to be genuine it must be spontaneous.

This segment's spirit of trying to do its best without martyring itself makes it effective at avoiding depression. A sense of time and urgency is usually lacking. It is extrememly relaxed.

It desires to fit all thoughts (of both itself and others), into one large and ever-expanding complex. It loves to learn and its interests are broad.

This segment, at worst, presents an air of superficiality because as long as there is new territory for it to cover it feels impelled to move on.

Usually there is a love of reading and of travel, and a desire to communicate with a variety of people. It will typically function more smoothly later in life when experiences have been collected upon which it may draw.

The Tarot: Sagittarius (The Conquerer, #7) combines with Gemini (The Star, #17) to produce Venus (The Two Paths, #6). Hence, the victor who is faithful to his higher nature, and who allows himself to be a

137

channel for higher entities may completely avoid temptation and achieve an awareness of true love.

Sagittarius 10°-12½° *Cancer:*

This segment likes to seek dubious, difficult, or dangerous tasks for itself. It likes to discover what is hidden. It has insatiable curiosity.

This segment is greatly psychosomatic. Its accomplishments depend heavily on its own self-image and estimation of its abilities. It may often become involved in psychicism and mediumship. It wants to be in control of natural forces through the exercise of its mental powers. It should stay away from drugs and impure substances.

It would rather attempt a Gargantuan task with little possibility of success than a small task which would yield less reward. It is capable of being persistent in its work and will effectively weather periods of adversity.

It may try things which it senses are not good for it, just to gain more experience. It feels that danger can only be conquered if it is met head on. It will not protect itself from peril because it feels that problems must be solved in a direct manner. Rather than put off unpleasant things, it will swiftly seek them out so as to be done with them. It would rather suffer its hardships in the present than have to deal with them later.

It may be defensive about its philosophy of life.

The Tarot: Sagittarius (The Conquerer, #7) combines with Cancer (The Moon, #18) to produce Sagittarius (The Conquerer, #7). Hence, true victory lies in becoming aware of one's instincts: those things which are hidden yet part on oneself. Each entity carries within itself the seeds of this victory.

Sagittarius 12½°-15° *Leo:*

The joy of evolving. This segment likes to exercise its abilities in actual processes. It tends to be highly ego-centric and intent on self-mastery. It takes things personally. It is happiest when having arrived at a long sought-after goal, and it is never content with itself as it is. It always wants to be improving and expanding — conquering new territory inside itself, but still building firmly on the groundwork of its past accomplishments.

It acts with surety, and is one of the most audacious segments of the zodiac. Courage is its natural asset, and it continually tests this asset.

There is a strong need to succeed here, and this segment should believe so completely in itself that failure does not bother it. It responds acutely to positive reinforcement and is less likely than most to become programmed adversely by negativity. Successes have a solidifying effect on its character.

Positively it has a flair for knowing its own limits and keeping within them. On the other hand it may fall into a habit of repeating itself rather than trying anything new.

It can overcome adversity through projecting a positive self-image.

The Tarot: Sagittarius (The Conquerer, #7) combines with Leo (The Sun, #19) to produce Capricorn (The Balance, #8). Hence, true victory implies a marriage to higher principles, and if this marriage is consummated, one's position as victor is solidified.

Sagittarius 15°-17½° *Virgo:*

This segment is a natural scientist, experimentor or inventor. It is interested in applying formulas to problems as a means of solving them. It can often analyze the same thing in two different ways and come up with different conclusions. It wants complete definitions which will encompass both what the thing is and what the thing is not. It is always in the process of re-understanding, with the idea that when understanding is complete, it may have control. There is a tendency here to specialize and to find new ways to apply old techniques. It is adept at dealing with the fine points of theories and abstractions.

This segment is a natural efficiency expert. It loves simple and effective solutions to problems. It wants to be successful without wasting motion.

It may have problems making up its mind. It believes in the idea of adequate preparation and is always in search of the best tools to accomplish its ends. It gains much experience from re-doing things, and is often unconcerned about how long it takes to do a project to its satisfaction.

After completion of a project it is very aware of flaws and it would rather go back and deal with these than go on to something new.

The Tarot: Sagittarius (The Conquerer, #7) combines with Virgo (Veiled Isis, #2) to produce Aquarius (The Sage, #9). Hence victorious domination of mind over matter will produce wisdom. It is aware of how to deny evil, but also to affirm good and by doing so, to make it real.

Sagittarius 17½°-20° *Libra:*

This segment wants to win, but it does not necessarily want anyone else to lose. It is like the military leader, who, after conquering, is benign in his attitude towards the vanquished and wants to rebuild the destruction he has caused. It wants to share its victory with others.

Its nature is restless. It busies itself with a number of projects simultaneously. It is resourceful in its manner of finding solutions to problems. It can invent tools and materials when the right ones for the job are lacking.

It makes a lot of plans, and when it can vividly envision its goal it is spurred to action. When unsure of its goal it will tend to put things off.

This segment is in need of strong motivation. It must feel a sense of purpose before it can produce. It does not usually function well in a position of servitude unless this position is temporary, as in apprenticeship.

The Tarot: Sagitarius (The Conquerer, #7) combines with Libra (Isis Unveiled, #3) to produce Uranus (The Wheel, #10). Hence, victory which is fruitful and productive must seek new and unique forms of attack on problems. Plans may be set, but their manifestation is often eccentric and liable to change.

Sagittarius 20°-22½° *Scorpio:*

This segment is concerned with the use of its own personal power, which it may fear. It experiences sudden and far-reaching moments of truth at the completion of goals. It is a very good judge of itself, sometimes too good. It feels a drive to fulfill its desires.

It wants to gain complete control of itself, but not in just a passive manner. It needs to be able to work with its inner forces rather than just know how to keep them in check.

It can often encounter intense moral conflicts when it doesn't live up to its self-image.

It wants victory over itself, and its goals are quite elusive. It will choose difficult and unique tasks and for this reason may need to work independently.

As an artist it can strike a tenuous balance between technical discipline and freedom of expression. It is adept at producing striking impressions which transcend their media.

The Tarot: Sagittarius (The Conquerer, #7) combines with Scorpio (The Sovereign, #4) to produce Neptune (The Enchantress, #11). Hence, when the natural dominion of spirit over matter is realized fully, spiritual power is instantly granted as an infinite resource.

Sagittarius 22½°-25° *Sagittarius:*

Success here is a state of mind. When this segment wants something, it wants it now.

It tends to desire what it can achieve. It may also dream of the unobtainable, but it is well aware that it is fantasy. Because of its practical attitude towards its desires, it will be let down less than most other segments. Sagittarius is an expansive sign and this segment loves to grow and develop and be aware of its own progress. It dislikes a feeling of solidified victory and will get bored easily after it has won.

It goes through changes in a kaleidoscopic manner. It likes to throw things together dynamically, such as divergent personalities and experience their opposing forces. It loves movement — anything kinetic.

Sagittarius is the sign of victory, and victory here is at its most innocent and subjective. It boils down to truly "doing one's own thing" and directly receiving forces from within and transforming them into action — to see what happens.

The Tarot: Sagittarius (The Conquerer, #7) combines with Sagittarius (The Conquerer, #7) to produce Taurus (The Alchemist, #14). Hence, loss and gain are ongoing processes, and to envision a win in the future takes the mind off the present so that one has failed in the True Goal before starting. Being victorious implies constant regeneration.

Sagittarius 25°-27½° *Capricorn:*

Seeing justification in all that it looks upon is the desire of this segment. It attempts this by isolating a particular part of a vision and then holding this part still in its mind. The expansive qualities of Sagittarius are here tempered by Capricorn caution. The result is an enthusiasm which is well-grounded in reality and not easily shaken. This segment is sure of its ability to accomplish so long as its motives and plans are in order.

It is interested not only in being victorious, but also in maintaining victory. This implies goals which are constantly being extended to protect the original goal from being lost. It wants to hold onto its happiness. What it needs to learn most is that constant change is the rule, and that even though safe-guards are wise, they are never a promise of security.

It seeks to turn its visions into realities. Its imagination is usally sensual. It is extremely serious about its personal beliefs and feels a need to take a moral stand on every issue. It would reject any philosophical argument which it felt was not workable on a practical basis.

The Tarot: Sagittarius (The Conquerer, #7) combines with Capricorn (The Balance, #8) to produce Saturn (The Black Magician, #15). Hence victory must eventually achieve a state of equillibrium to be lasting.

Sagittarius 27½°-30° *Aquarius:*

A winning nature is sure to be found here. This segment is indomitable. It learns swiftly from experience and will be ready to try again. It barely admits the possibility of failure, because failure is a telling experience; contained in the experience is the reason why one failed and therefore the key to future success.

This segment develops its philosophy of life very simply from experience. This segment is not likely to rationalize in favor of itself, but rather takes an objective view which is also non-egotistical. Its approach to life is in the manner of Zen. It perceives and therefore it knows, but the knowing is one with the perception rather than an aftermath.

This segment is interested in what is, as a total experience. It feels that philosophy is immediate and palpable.

It will play with ideas rather than taking them

seriously. It has a unique flair for making connections between divergent branches of knowledge.

We might call it the segment of "philosophical openness."

The Tarot: Sagittarius (The Conquerer, #7) combines with Aquarius (The Sage, #9) to produce Mars (The Lightning, #16). Hence victory won through the force of wisdom is a powerful equalizer, and reveals the truth that all life and existence is one . . . "She never stumbles, she's got no place to fall . . . She knows theres no success like failure, and that failure's no success at all." (Bob Dylan).

Capricorn 0°-2½° *Aquarius:*

Capricorn, the sign of the solidification of spirit into matter, begins with a segment having Aquarius subrulership. This symbolizes that the purpose of physical reality is like a vehicle for the growth and development of wisdom (Aquarius = "I know"). This segment learns from experience. It is effective at applying what it knows on a practical level. It sets reasonable goals for itself and works toward them.

It is exacting in its search for reasons. It will adhere to codes of conduct only if it is sure of their purpose. It wants to be able to explain itself if called upon to do so.

It will never choose the new or the old merely because it is new or old, but will approach everything with as little bias as possible. It will re-try things which it has been told are tried and true and will investigate things which common consent has labeled invalid or useless.

It is in search of an eternal code by which to live,

and this will keep it from making snap judgments. Its goal is perfect self-realization. It likes to do things to see what sort of a reaction it will get.

The Tarot: Capricorn (The Balance #8) combines with Aquarius (The Sage, #9) to produce Gemini (The Star, #17). Hence justice meted out with wisdom becomes a medium of expression for higher intelligence, and is the means of raising that which is below.

Capricorn 2½°-5° *Pisces:*

This segment feels a strong need to dedicate itself to specific habits and thereby bring a certain set routine into its existence. It adheres to the rules that it sets for itself, arbitrary as these may be. It wants to possess a style.

It dedicates itself to objectivity and tries to get outside itself so it may clearly see the difference between its conscious reasoning processes and its biases.

It is immediately aware of the dangers and pitfalls of being inconsistent and wants to see everything from a viewpoint which is definite in the stand that it takes. It may see other people's points of view, and though it is accepting of other opinions, it wants to remain unswerving in its own judgments.

This segment is completely self-accepting. It does not want to change. It feels a sense of duty to maintain what it is. It weathers catastrophies well, and a strong death wish may even be present. This need not be pathological though, since this segment is innately aware of the inevitability of redemption. It wants to do its suffering now so that it will not have to do it later.

It is often quite sensuous and may feel chained to

146

matter, but it does not kick against this bondage. Its attitude is acceptance of its desires while believing in a promise of something higher.

At worst it may feel trapped by its own reactions.

The Tarot: Capricorn (The Balance, #8) combines with Pisces (The Martyr, #12) to produce the Moon (The Sacrophagus, #20). Hence, asserting to everything as being part of one's own personal karma is the means of working it out and thereby attaining complete consciousness.

Capricorn 5°-7½° *Aries:*

All events, though seemingly chance, have meaning to this segment. It will be naturally transformed by these "chances" which affect it. It will attempt to build something, to put energy into a structure, but if the wind blows this structure away, it is likely to ask itself why, rather than asking the wind. It is open to learning and will take an interest in any knowledge which comes its way, assured that there is reason and purpose behind random patterns.

This segment is effective at capitalizing on the pioneer efforts of others, organizing and crystallizing new ideas. It would rather extend and amplify pre-established ideas than come up with new ones. There may be nothing new under the sun, but for it there can be old things waiting to be rediscovered and re-used.

Awareness comes through re-ordering. This segment learns by re-arranging what it already knows. It is always seeking definition. It wants exactitude in its work. It is persuaded by clear, sound thinking, and by logical arguments unclouded by details or side issues.

Its creativity will usually select conventional patterns through which to express itself.

147

The Tarot: Capricorn (The Balance, #8), combines with Aries (The Reaper, #13) to produce the Sun (The Adept, #21). Hence, justice adheres to laws, but when justice has power to transform, then complete fulfillment of the Divine Will can be attained.

Capricorn 7½°-10° *Taurus:*

Typified here is Capricorn's most conservative aspect. This segment is a maintainer of the status quo and is highly suspicious of anything which attempts a fast overthrow of pre-existing circumstances. It sees change correctly being effected by growth which is gradual rather than by cataclysm.

Structure is all-important and therefore it may experience much anxiety during change due to being placed in an unprotected position.

This segment is effective at getting a maximum amount of mileage out of a minimum amount of fuel because it organizes itself along practical lines. It is, at best, impeccably reliable and consistently responsible.

It thinks of progression in terms of repairing or adjusting the old rather than of creating the new out of new materials.

This segment is a veritable rock and will often attract others who will lean on it. In undeveloped types, this can result in using others due to their dependency.

It will strive to be independent. It isn't concerned about taking care of other people, but it wants to be capable of taking care of itself. This desire to be self-regenerating can often manifest as a grabbiness or hoarding of resources. In evolved entities it will show up as a disregard for anything physical, and self-fulfillment through becoming unattached to anything

148

material; in other words, an independence which is spiritually transcendent.

Often this segment is distrustful of drugs or medicines when it becomes sufficiently enlightened to see that they can be made unnecessary through force of consciousness.

The Tarot: Capricorn (The Balance, #8) combines with Taurus (The Alchemist, #14) to produce Pluto (The Materialist, #22). Hence, equillibrium which is self-regenerating and tempered presents an irresistable force which is either blindly materialistic or else the pinnacle of spiritual power.

Capricorn 10°-12½° *Gemini:*

A deep-set sense of optimism is found here. This segment is busily attempting to set aright everything with which it comes into contact. It wants to turn everything to practical account, and to reduce things to basic and logical patterns.

It believes in an ideal and perfect justice which is beyond time and space, but it also realizes that practical considerations cannot always be brought into perfect attunement with this. Therefore the Gemini vibration, which is dualistic, manifests in this segment as being at once completely idealistic and yet compromising and flexible.

The secret which this segment must karmically manifest to others is that the nature of perfect truth cannot ever be betrayed. Purity is its own protection, and purity (so-called) which is capable of being torn down or tempted was never truly pure to begin with.

The most negative aspect of this segment is that it can become outwardly amoral by thinking of its motives or intentions as pure on the one hand while committing acts which oppose this morality on the other. This segment can be too forgiving of itself; too quick to give itself a second chance and thereby to fall into a rut of never-ending second chances.

The Tarot: Capricorn (The Balance, #8) combines with Gemini (The Star, #17) to produce Sagittarius (The Conquerer, #7). Hence justice achieves victory through being ever faithful to its own personal sense of right and wrong.

Capricorn 12½°-15° *Cancer:*

Structure most usually implies a delimitation, but here is a driving force to make structure all-inclusive, so that no laws need ever be disproven, and the rules are general enough to never have exceptions.

At root this segment tends to see the cosmos as a womb of infinite proportion.

Other people tend to project their own image on it. It tends not to be what it seems. It may seem to be a dependent type when actually it is very independent.

It is completely accepting of itself, but will probably need to find time alone so that it does not become caught up in the problems and ideas of others.

In the arts it is often capable of masterful deception or illusion, because it knows how to distort through juxtaposition. It is adept at finding positive uses for things which are negative or worthless. It is capable of highly persuasive arguments, and of making any concept seem valid.

This segment is acutely aware of its own invisible conditioning and is therefore very sensitive to what it exposes itself. It knows that anything it comes into contact with will exert an influence on it.

The Tarot: Capricorn (The Balance, #8) combines with Cancer (The Moon, #18) to produce Capricorn (The Balance, #8). Hence structure which is cosmic is only itself, neither containing nor contained. Awareness is that which calls it heaven or hell, and thereby makes it that.

Capricorn 15°-17½° *Leo:*

Joy of individual effort best expresses the meaning of this segment. It is happiest when at work. It loves to organize, to find a place for everything and have everything in its place. It manifests its creativity through choosing an order of things already existing rather than inventing anything completely new.

This segment has a constant impulse to do things in its own unique way, but is often quite set in these unique ways. Any difficulty it meets on the outer plane is an obvious reflection of its inner state. It will truly convince itself of the purity of its motives by putting them into action. It believes the notion that one does not really know something until they have tried it, so it is quite intent on gratifying its own desires in a tangible way.

It believes in situational morality, in that it makes its judgments in the light of the particular circumstances surrounding a situation rather than to consult general laws. It can be decisive in its criticisms. It changes its mind only slowly and carefully, and is happiest when its attitudes do not have to be amended. It becomes irritated with anything which is

151

ambiguous because it feels everything can ultimately be made definite.

The Tarot: Capricorn (The Balance, #8) combines with Leo (The Sun, #19) to produce Aquarius (The Sage, #9). Hence, complete crystallization of personality should imply complete self-knowledge, or ultimate wisdom.

Capricorn 17½°-20° *Virgo:*

The function here is one of achieving pure balance and finding a means of crystallizing to perfection a system or doctrine.

This is the segment of analytical judgment.

This segment wants to order and objectify anything which is hidden and mysterious, not to rob it of its mystery, but to make the mystery self-evident.

This segment is capable of grasping situations quickly and acting with expediency. Servitude comes easily if convinced it will reap rewards from its labor.

It is apt to work at length on a project, refining it as much as possible with more interest in the clarity of the product than in its completion.

It is quite concerned over details. It sees minutiae as contributing to a whole and therefore as something potentially distracting from the overall impression. There is a quality of "not being able to see the forest for the trees." Operating on a more positive level, it will produce a one-pointed insight which is capable of catching and undoing snags.

The Tarot: Capricorn (The Balance) #8), combines with Virgo (Veilled Isis, #2) to produce Uranus (The Wheel, #10). Hence structure which is based on scien-

152

tific knowledge must explain everything from two angles: action and reaction. Projecting a structure on nature implies analyzing things from a multiplicity of different viewpoints.

Capricorn 20°-22½° *Libra:*

Capricorn here is at its most fruitful. This segment is a hard and diligent worker. It is not one to get hung up in the petty details of its work. It wants to see the job get done. This segment will do anything it can to keep a project underway. In marriage, it will often do anything to save the relationship from divorce.

It has a deep set notion that it is here to do a job or else it would not be here; and if it is not completely sure as to what that job is, it will work at what is immediate until it finds out.

Hidden connections between divergent lines of endeavor are easily seen. There is a wide variety of roads that can be taken to a single destination. Goals are either short range, or each step to them is felt subjectively as a partial completion of the task. This segment yearns to be productive, and therefore needs to have its product clearly defined, at least in its own mind.

The impulse behind this segment is one of giving birth directly rather than of nurturing. For this reason any children or creations which are produced are not dwelt on in retrospect, but are weaned as soon as possible to make way for gestation of other concepts or ideas.

Not much faith is put into abstractions or potentials. This segment feels that accomplishment must start with the act of accepting a possibility and reject-

153

ing others so that something tangible may manifest.

The Tarot: Capricorn (the Balance, #8) combines with Libra (Isis Unveilled, #3) to produce Neptune (The Enchantress, #11). Hence equillibrium to be truly balanced, must be dynamic and constantly re-orienting itself. This is true spiritual power.

Capricorn 22½°-25° *Scorpio:*

A desire to dominate best characterizes this segment. It will seek out stable situations — circumstances which hold it down, or which have a confining effect on it. When these are obtained, it usally comes to a crises of awareness, and there is a resulting desire to break out of its bonds.

This segment is a cautious and secretive planner. It is actualy aware of its own shortcomings. It takes for granted that it gets what it deserves. Its thoughts are directed toward the understanding and realization of justice. It summarizes events as they are in the present and wants to categorize them all. Its moral sense is strong, and it wants to do what is right.

Its acts are consistently based on emotions. Since it sees two sides of an issue, or two ways in which a problem can be solved, it chooses the way it feels to be correct.

This segment operates best in the here and now. It does not fare so well in dealing with abstract concepts, because it needs sound concrete reality in order to function, so it can be aware of its motives. It is concerned with understanding the forces of the material world in order to gain power over them. It needs to realize that material interests are a binding influence and that on the relative plane, all blessings carry curses and all curses carry blessings. Its karma lies in its attitude towards its own personal freedom, for it is here that its problems are worked out.

The Tarot: Capricorn (The Balance, #8) combines with Scorpio (The Soveriegn, #4) to produce Pisces (The Martyr, #12). Hence, any crystallization of desire into tangilble reality brings a realization of the self's imprisonment in matter, and out of this realization is born subtler and more evolutionary desires.

Capricorn 25°-27½° *Sagittarius:*

This is a segment of repairs. It revitablizes old, established concepts rather than seeking new ones. It wins out through sticking persistently to a single course of action. It is intent on self-discipline and is constantly attempting to tame itself so that it may make effective use of what it has.

It wants to succeed in a material sense. It is desirous of securing its position in the world, and the act of stabilizing its lot in life is an endlessly ongoing process. This segment's effectiveness depends on how efficiently organized it can become.

Sexual involvements cause it to expand in awareness, because of an acute sensitivity to its own physical mechanism. Negatively, this segment may be quite selfish, but its total self-concern can manifest positively as a constructive self-interest. As it improves itself, it raises the vibrations of its immediate environment and those which come into contact with it.

This segment may wear itself out through its one-pointedness. It is boldly persistent, even when it knows it cannot win, and this doggedness tends to wear away slowly and inexorably anything which is impure within itself.

The Tarot: Capricorn (The Balance, #8) combines with Sagittarius (The Conquerer, #7) to produce Saturn (The Black Magician, #15). Hence, when the forces and crystallization are victorious, predestination becomes a reality.

Capricorn 27½°-30° *Capricorn:*

This segment is compromising only when it needs to be. It lets nothing stand in its way. If it meets an obstacle, it will simply rechart its course. Its solution to problems is direct and practical. It can handle dangerous situations with skill.

Its stability is deep and unseen, usually aligned to accepted or traditional values. It has a talent for knowing what is socially proper.

Sex represents a powerful force. Often its desires are potent and direct, but it is capable of exercising great self-control. Its attraction to another person is strong and constant.

This segment is good at arranging things. It has a fine sense of form, and wants to do its best with what it has. Its understanding of design is innate.

It may seem at times unmerciful, or uncompassionate towards other people. This stems from an emotional nature which is forceful though often impersonal. Emotional energy is consciously contained and the force of this containment tends to make it more effective when let loose. This ability to contain the raw energy of self makes this segment capable of sustained patience.

This segment's greatest virtue is its ability to cope

with crises. It is very much in tune with its unconscious and seems to be able to call up enough inner resources to handle any situation.

The Tarot: Capricorn (The Balance, #8) combines with Capricorn (The Balance, #8) to produce Mars (The Lightning, #16). Hence equilibrium is a dynamic state. True balance is flexible.

Aquarius 0°-2½° *Capricorn:*

This segment likes to learn a number of different skills. Its selection of friends is often based on the same professional interest. Reality can force it to be practical, but this is usually felt as a limitation. It thinks logically more than it acts logically. It is open-minded and deliberate in its thoughts. It makes a reliable friend and expects the same.

This segment employs abstract concepts in an immediate manner. It does not relate easily to any idea which is too far removed from reality. Reason reaches its ultimate high point as a tool. The two signs combined here reveal the conflict between the two sides of Saturn: formal structure, as in a blueprint, and practical structure, as in the material work completed from the blueprint. Changes often have to be made when theory is put into practice. This problem is the main concern of this segment. It often will judge others in theory but forgive them in practice, proving that the most workable structure is the one which can grow, departing from its original form, but only in its feasibility and never in spirit.

The Tarot: Aquarius (The Sage, #9) combines with Capricorn (The Balance, #8) to produce Gemini (The

157

Star, #17). Hence the Sage sees truth as relative and will be a medium for the force of evolution, even if this means living what men call lies, or acting in a manner which laws deem unjust. Pure truth is always an exception to a rule.

Aquarius 2½°-5° *Aquarius:*
Here faith becomes strong enough to be called knowledge. This segment is very sure about what it knows. It has a powerful Utopian dream — equality for everyone. Friends are all-important to this segment, although it tends to respond to people more on a collective than an individual level.

This segment may display a lack of accomplishment, due to an idealistic approach to the execution of plans. It is adept at visualizing things, without material aids. It is much more effective as an advisor than one who actually carries out a project. It is open to learning and may collect such things as books.

It may be accused of being emotionally cold. This stems from its highly developed sense of encountering everything through the mind. At root it is brave because it knows that all questions have answers. Since these answers are contained in the questions, everything has a solution.

It is prudent and cannot be forced to make fast decisions. However its decisions may at times be fast indeed, as if inspired by some divine source which graces it with solutions at the speed of electricity.

The Tarot: Aquarius (The Sage, #9) combines with Aquarius (The Sage, #9) to produce Cancer (The Moon, #18). Hence, the Sage in his purity has accumulated so much experience that he may brave the abyss innocently without danger.

Aquarius 5°-7½° *Pisces:*

This is one of the most open-minded of all the segments. It searches for universal truths and dedicates itself to living by what it feels to be right. It is intent on understanding why people believe as they do. It accepts the necessity for faith, but wants to find out where this necessity comes from; that is, what inner motives cause it.

This segment displays a marked talent for "reading" its own intuitions. It excels in self-analysis. It likes to figure out other people and generally does not judge.

It feels a responsibility towards learning, but this needn't mean gathering facts through books or other traditional means. This segment often learns by perceiving phenomena and drawing conclusions from them. It may manifest a lack of selectivity: it is ready to investigate anything that comes its way. Its primary motive is to draw conclusions from what it experiences without moralizing. It is not much interested in the ethics of a situation. This does not mean that it is amoral but that it views morals as a matter of personal preference.

The Tarot: Aquarius (The Sage, #9) combines with Pisces (The Martyr, #12) to produce the Sun (The Adept, #21). Hence, the Sage, possessing inner strength, dedicates this strength to a cause, and thereby completes himself.

Aquarius 7½°-10° *Aries:*

This segment is continuously beginning anew in the mind. Lack of prudence produces failure which in turn produces wisdom. It is fast to give itself and others a second chance.

What anyone knows or has experienced changes them, and this law is more purely appreciated in this segment than in others.

It sees the future as a promise, and even though the promise may be chaos, there is an awareness that nothing is permanent. For this segment, the concept of constant change is a source of security.

It likes to change its mind and enlarge its thoughts. It does not give up easily. Often, rather than make decisions, it will allow itself to float freely in circumstances to "see what will happen." It likes to put itself in unusual environments to find out what new ideas or relationships will evolve. It enjoys trying the untried, and will usually set challenging goals for itself.

Negatively, it tends to test itself, and often continues this testing until it fails. There can be a need to lose here. This can, however, lead to a firm re-grasp of the situation.

This segment is only as careful as it needs to be without straining itself. With much experience it can evolve into a state of secure and relaxed wisdom.

The Tarot: Aquarius (The Sage, #9) combines with Aries (The Reaper, #13) to produce Pluto (The Materialist, #22). Hence, wisdom in its aspect of dynamic transformation penetrates the unseen world and becomes an irresistable force.

Aquarius 10°-12½° *Taurus:*

This segment desires to make knowledge its own. It possesses knowledge by putting it into a structure, and as the knowledge grows, it expands and reforms the structure out of necessity.

This segment often follows set patterns of thinking and it feels secure when it has rules to go by. It wants to make plans and then follow them closely. It is often accused of being set in its ways. Its basic attitude is, "I will continue in my present course, and will not change it until I find something better."

It is slow to be convinced, but once it is, rarely changes its mind. It is staunchly loyal.

This segment is a builder of ideas. It treats thoughts as things. It is good at making less mean more; that is, reasoning in a manner which is persuasive due to a clear and simple approach.

It is mentally conservative. It wants to accumulate knowledge and likes to listen to knowledgable people, but it does not like to think, unless there is some goal in mind or some problem to be solved. In this manner it conserves its own mental energy.

It tends to be stubborn in the pursuit of its goals.

The Tarot: Aquarius (The Sage, #9) combines with Taurus (The Alchemist, #14) to produce Jupiter (The Hierophant, #5). Hence wisdom which exercises temperence can triumph over matter through harmonizing it.

Aquarius 12½°-15° *Gemini:*

This segment is quite liberal in its thinking. It is a hopeful planner. In a group it takes on multiple roles and may try to be everything to everyone. It likes to be a messenger — a collector and disseminator of facts and knowledge. It tends to have a lot of friends and to present sharply differing facets of itself to different people.

161

Its mind is adept at dealing with abstractions and it is quick to give advice. It searches for laws and precepts which will hold true in any situation. It is sure that these laws exist, and will strive to find them. It can contradict itself without knowing or caring. It tends to be spontaneous and intuitive in its realizations.

It tends to put knowledge together from a variety of sources, in the manner of a collage. It is receptive to any facts it might glean, but tends to read into these facts its own meaning. It seeks to be true to itself.

The Tarot: Aquarius (The Sage, #9), combines with Gemini (The Star #17) to produce Capricorn (The Balance, #8). Hence, wisdom is not something apart from reality, but grows out of it, just as a plant produces a flower.

Aquarius 15°-17½° *Cancer:*

This segment attempts to journey backwards to the root of all ideas to see where knowledge comes from. It nurtures and protects concepts.

Much indulgence in fantasy is to be found here. It likes to search out hidden knowledge in dangerous places. When it discovers concepts, it attempts to project its feelings of awe and wonder for these concepts onto others. It feels a deep affinity with ancient knowledge.

This segment has definite ideas on a visceral level, but it has difficulty finding means to communicate these ideas to others. This segment lives in a private world of the imagination. It feels its wisdom welling up from some primal source.

Pantheism is often found here; specifically, a feeling that truth is a product of consciousness on a cellular

162

level. Aquarius desires to make all equal, and in this case the desire is approached through Cancer, the primordial water sign which is the matrix of life in its organic aspect. Biological blueprints are, to this segment, like books of ancient knowledge. It feels deep affinities with plants and animals.

The Tarot: Aquarius (The Sage, #9) combines with Cancer (The Moon, #18) to produce Aquarius (The Sage, #9). Hence, the Sage is the Sage because he has completely explored his own subconscious. The true Sage always was, is and will be that. He crosses the abyss of the unknown totally unchanged.

Aquarius 17½°-20° *Leo:*

Other people mean much to this segment. It loves others for their individuality, and strives to bring this quality out in anyone that it meets. It attempts to emphasize harmony between people. It wants itself as well as others to stand out in a group. The only qualities which unite it to others are motives of the most broad and general sort, usually love and protection.

It feels that any two people can get along. If it must do something which will cause conflict, it will do it in the most surreptitious manner.

It likes to work alone and yet desires its labor to effect others. It is drawn to anything which is unique and personal — an individual's manifestation of universality.

It has great need for privacy so that it can be itself, yet without feeling that it is functioning in a vaccuum. The bonds between itself and others are strong, and ideally, non-limiting.

The Tarot: Aquarius (The Sage, #9) combines with

Leo (The Sun, #19) to produce Uranus (The Wheel, #10). Hence the Sage is the embodiment of universal laws, but he is also an individual existing in time and space. This releases him from the disturbing influences of constant change, because he is both transcendently strong and resiliant.

Aquarius 20°-22½° *Virgo:*

This is a research segment. It collects scientific data, and from this data forms unique conclusions. It is interested in the logical or philosophical implications of techniques. It is effective in making detailed plans. In a group or community it will take on the role of a servant who organizes the peripheral details. Envisioning a central goal motivates it to be industrious. It loves to render services for friends.

It learns by experience. Often its dealings with others are secretive. It shows aptitude for manipulating people, due to its innate understanding of group mechanics.

It is concerned with what knowledge is, and wonders how it knows what it knows. It wants to know things from multiple angles. This naturally leads it to becoming an authority.

If the rest of the chart points to a broader scattering of energies, this segment is at least aware of what it knows.

This segment tries to standardize its thinking through relating it to patterns which are unique and complex. It is often verbose in its explanations, and at worst can confuse itself as well as others.

The Tarot: Aquarius (The Sage, #9) combines with Virgo (Veiled Isis, #2) to produce Neptune (The En-

164

chantress, #11). Hence when wisdom researches the laws of nature, which are the hidden substructures of reality, it is led to the brink of the unseen world. The Sage whose understanding is complete has collected and organized factual information through experience and has ultimately refined his senses so that he may tune in to a higher cosmic order in which all life lives, moves and breathes.

Aquarius 22½°-25° *Libra:*

This segment strives to work with others. It is always ready to compromise in the present, and hopes that its ideals will not need to be compromised in the future. It wants to build its blueprints — to infuse its ideas into a material form. It has a genius for using other people's best talents, and for drawing them out. It is friendly and diplomatic and has no trouble fitting into groups.

It neither looks up to nor down on people. It encounters everyone as equal in terms of their humanity. It senses that talent is a function of individuality, and that each person has talents specific to themselves which must be discovered and improved upon. It is quite open to the influence of others. Its hopes and wishes usually hinge on partnerships and joint efforts.

The sign Aquarius has been accused of mental problem solving without concrete action to back it up. This segment has this quality less than any other in Aquarius. It sees wisdom as something which, because of its power, has an outward effect. If wisdom does not or cannot manifest in deed, then it is not true wisdom.

The Tarot: Aquarius (The Sage, #9) combines with

Libra (Isis Unveiled, #3) to produce Pisces (The Martyr, #12). Hence, wisdom manifested in action implies dedication, and the acceptance of responsibility for acts.

Aquarius 25°-27½° *Scorpio:*

This segment has great powers of thought and attempts to make everything within itself conscious. It wants to know, and shows complete willingness to learn. It likes exchanging ideas, and wants to know the truth. It attempts to mete out its idea of justice in a tangible manner.

It approaches experience objectively and is revitalized by new involvements. It conserves its energy. In criticizing others it will often experience sudden self-knowledge.

This segment is in danger of becoming inactive due to its rumination and its love of beginning anew.

It is intrigued by paradoxes, and strives to see all sides of things. It desires to form its own ideas, and reacts negatively to anyone who tries to take control. It dislikes biases, unless they are admitted as such. It sees everyone as a potential teacher.

It shies away from the idea of fate, and wants to exercise its free will.

It has a flair for research work and is adept at working out problems and figuring out riddles. It approaches life as if it were a puzzle.

The Tarot: Aquarius (The Sage,#9) combines with Scorpio (The Sovereign, #4) to produce Aries (The Reaper, #13). Hence, the thinking process produces wisdom which has direct transforming power on life.

166

"We shape our tools and then our tools shape us."
(Marshall McLuhan).

Aquarius 27½°-30° *Sagittarius:*

This segment personifies mind over matter. It is interested in material concerns, from the standpoint of trying to find a way to dominate them. Out of this is borne a natural bent for philosophy. It wants true understanding apart from material proof or inductive reasoning. It attempts to answer questions.

It is capable of extremely careful thought and approaches problems squarely with the intellect. Mental exhaustion can set in when answers are hard to find, because when this segment is intent on a solution, it does not give up.

It can be self-righteous about its own ideas. Its philosophy of life often tends towards dogma which it will uphold no matter what. It is more aware of the workings of its own mind than of anything outside itself, hence its perceptions are usually abstract. It may have difficulty in self-expression unless the vocabulary is large and the education liberal.

There is a tenuous balance here between being careful and being audacious. The carefulness is more in effect, but to such an extent that it becomes audacity: this segment cannot and will not be pushed by circumstances. It moves at its own self-regulated pace, and this is its boldness.

The Tarot: Aquarius (The Sage, #9) combines with Sagittarius (The Conquerer, #7) to produce Mars (The Lightning, #16). Hence, wisdom becomes relentless and in so doing, tests itself or its obstacle to the breaking point. Right knowledge is the mainstream of evolution, and represents an irresistible force.

Pisces 0°-2½° *Sagittarius:*

This segment is the beginning of the end, the dissolution which is the function of the sign Pisces. This dissolution begins with expansion, a dissolving through opening and spreading apart, like a flower. This segment clings to a core of established beliefs and extends itself from this core in all directions while still connected to it.

Sympathy and understanding for others is usually present. Expansion is multilateral, and there are so many thoughts and plans in the stage of gestation that some of them must be abandonded to allow others to flourish. Choosing the area in which energy will be expended is not easy. This segment does things in extremes. Idealism becomes removed as far as possible from material reality. It is prone to sudden flashes of the complete synergistic inner-connections of reality; seeing exalted realms in the here and now. Often there is difficulty verbalizing these cognitions. This segment is prone to hallucinations. It can loose itself through its imagination.

Disappointments are usually due to unrealized ideals. Over-doing is this segment's undoing. The thinking is highly abstract.

The Tarot: Pisces (The Martyr, #12) and Sagittarius (The Conquerer, #7) combine to produce Leo (The Sun, #19). Pisces becomes inspired, and is capable of unselfishness. There is a desire to be magnanimous. Negatively, this may lead to delusions of grandeur.

168

Pisces 2½°-5° *Capricorn:*

Sympathy (Pisces) reaches its most practical (Capricorn) point. This segment accepts everything it encounters. The assumption that life is based on a meaningful pattern is a key to this segment's nature. Any motive is seen as being potentially positive. The "lot in life" goes unquestioned. It is merely something to be worked out. The question "why me?" never occurs. When low energy periods occur, this segment knows intuitively that the only way to go is up.

Here is a natural inclination to take on responsibility, even if difficult. Karma is accepted subconsciously, whether this segment realizes it or not. Therefore, all bondage is met with submission and with the idea that when the debt is paid, liberation will follow as a natural course.

The energy here operates like dripping water wearing away rock. Softness and passivity become forceful assets because they are relentless.

This is a beneficial segment for parenthood, since its attitude towards personality conflicts is innocent and desirous of compromise.

The Tarot: Pisces (The Martyr, #12) combines with Capricorn (The Balance, #18) to produce the Moon (The Sacrophagus, #20). Here is constant reawakening to universal laws through encountering the limits of material reality. Also a drive to submit to present hardships as a means of fulfilling a future promise.

Pisces 5°-7½° *Aquarius:*

This segment produces unequivocal belief; an ability to withstand much pressure when it is sure. It feels that everything can be ultimately understood. Here is a deep desire for understanding among the members of a group — a will to be a part of something, and to penetrate the depths of personal relationships. This segment does not seek individuals to have intimate relationships but wants all relationships to be opening up so that more people can be accepted into a non-exclusive brotherhood.

This segment can scare others or make them angry because it does not respond to jealousy or territorial lines. There is fear of misunderstanding, not only by others but fear that people will misunderstnad each other. This segment doesn't crave privacy, and tears down synthetic barriers that others might think necessary. This can make it, at worst, shunned and at best, respected for its ability to be fearless in its dealings with others.

This segment sees itself in other people. It must be careful not to overshadow others with its self-projections. It tends to feel bonds of friendship as mystical and exalted. It is intent on making everyone equal through raising up the lowly.

There is difficulty putting thoughts into words. Plans are often vague, or tend to dissolve before they are realized.

The Tarot: Pisces (The Martyr, #12) combines with Aquarius (The Sage, #9) to produce the Sun (The Adept, #21). Hence, the Martyr is dedicated to seeking hidden supports and bringing to light hidden limitations so that they can be overcome.

Pisces 7½°-10° *Pisces:*

The main drive here is to be a martyr — to get lost in something, or someone, as a means of self-sacrifice. The problem is whether this will be a conscious attempt to give to something worthy, or an unconscious submitting to addiction. The will to believe is strong.

Food and drink have a powerful effect on this segment. Drugs have an especially adverse influence and they are often craved.

Romantic inclinations are intense and do not easily change course. Withdrawal of love through the breaking of a bond is something this segment fears.

There is a need to locate a still point in the midst of change. Although this segment is not adept at finding the shortest path to its goals, it is flowing towards them.

It has difficulty in experiencing anything from its surroundings. This can be beneficial for finding solutions to problems. Negatively, there is difficulty in seeing the core of a problem. Solutions are often located similar to the manner in which dowser finds water. Innate ability for psychic healing is present.

The Tarot: Pisces (The Martyr, #12) combines with Pisces (The Martyr, #12) to produce Venus (The Two Paths, #6). Hence, the Martyr becomes self-realized through love. (Venus is exalted in Pisces). He is either a slave to his passions, which is ultimately a selfish and self-destructive path, or he becomes a conscious and dedicated slave to something of value, and thereby aligns himself with the force of evolution.

Pisces 10°-12½° *Aries:*

This segment loves the unknown and approaches it exhuberantly, as an explorer would seek unmapped terriroty. Nothing is seen as impossible. It loves concepts which are either very old or very new. It often will "rediscover" an idea which it has had all along. It responds to the challenge of games where the odds are against it. Often there is a strong will to break through the bonds of conformity.

It becomes so mentally involved in things that there is little energy left to manifest its ideas concretely. Positively, when something is finally done, it is usually with great decisiveness.

This segment manifests devotion to a cause and is hopeful that the banner which it carries can transform the world. It attains much courage through this devotion. It is quick to sacrifice anything less valuable for what it believes in; it can be quite surprised when its ideals are not immediately accepted by others. It is intent on convincing others. It has a desire to lead an exemplary life — to practice what it preaches.

Self-fulfillment is gained through surrendering the self to the senses, and thereby learning their secrets — which is an ultimate key to self-control. (Blake's dictum: "The road of excess leads to the palace of wisdom").

The Tarot: Pisces (The Martyr, #12) combines with Aries (The Reaper, #13) to produce Sagittarius (The Conquerer, #7). Hence, submission to the continual flow of creation and destruction becomes a means of winning out over this unceasing process. Expansion of understanding is effected by giving in to the inevitability of change.

Pisces 12½°-15° *Taurus:*

Strength here is dependent on limits. The drive is toward systematizing the beliefs so that a dogma can be adhered to. This segment is successful in strengthening the faith of others by functioning in a manner which exemplifies its own ideals. It searches for an underlying consistency in all things. A self-imposed blindness to its own weaknesses may be present. Sympathy here is a struggle. Ideas once expressed are not easily given up, due to a fear of change. This segment wants to be a pillar in the ocean — capable of withstanding the highest waves without crumbling. In life it cautiously seeks strong waves to test and temper its strength. It has need of finding itself worthy. It advances and stops, but will rarely retreat.

This segment is a natural builder. It wants to build a labyrinth. Its goals may fail by being too detailed, or too all-encompassing.

Its greatest virtue is stability in the midst of difficulty.

The Tarot: Pisces (The Martyr, #12) combines with Taurus (The Alchemist, #14) to produce Capricorn (The Balance, #8). Hence, the Martyr, one who gives, has no recriminations about giving. He does not turn back, and because he acts with knowledge of his right action, he is regenerated.

Pisces 15°-17½° *Gemini:*

Here the two fish are held together with the longest possible tether. One explores the depths of the spring — the source of the river — while the other one attempts liberation from the river to the ocean.

Superficially, this segment seems completely irrational because of its cognizance of the unseen. Logic, to it, is a mirage — an excuse which may distort the truth.

The mind is active, but operates on such an elusive

level that ideas are expressed with great difficulty. There is often a tendency to overexplain things in an attempt to make them clear. Often it believes in two opposite things at once.

The learning process is highly individualistic, and needs to operate independently to be at its best. Faith here is truly blind, and therefore absolutely innocent. Upsets occur when people try to dissuade this segment from the course that it is following. This does not happen due to self-doubt, but because of a drive to make its motives known and understood by other people. It may have a naive assumption that everyone is as intensely interested in what it is doing as it is.

This segment signifies the communication of sympathy. It is capable of being in vivid rapport, on a feeling level, with all people around itself. To be self-fulfilled, it must maintain a clear sense of where its personal commitments lie.

This segment searches for ultimate truth in Being rather than in a balanced equation. Its ultimate interest is in content reduced to essence, rather than form.

The Tarot: Pisces (The Martyr, #12) combines with Gemini (The Star, #17) to produce Neptune (The Enchantress, #11). Hence, dedication to inner illumination, to oneself as one's own star, produces spiritual power. The individual aligns itself with its feelings, and by denying appearances, can see beyond the shroud of reason.

Pisces 17½°-20° *Cancer:*

Beliefs here have strong and usually obvious roots in the emotional makeup. This segment wants to lay itself open to the world and to be accepted for what it is. There is an uncontrollable desire to explore the self, especially in those aspects which may seem dangerous. Self-acceptance here is powerful, as well as its sister talent, self-protection.

This segment believes that anything can improve if given enough motherly care. For this reason there is difficulty in breaking off relationships even if it is causing pain. This is especially true if the other person appeals to its sympathy.

This segment operates almost solely on instinct. It wants a great deal of room in which to function. It does not want to be changed by what is outside itself. It would rather have self-transformation a self-enclosed process.

The drift here is always from the particular to the universal. It responds to all life sympathetically.

Privacy is extremely necessary here, but the concept of territory is subjective. This segment may feel that privacy is being usurped, but not be able to say why or how.

This segment could be called, "the defender of the faith."

The Tarot: Pisces (The Martyr, #12) combines with Cancer (The Moon, #18) to produce Libra (Isis Unveiled, #3). Hence, the Martyr feels so much intensity for his cause that he is in effect married to it. This emotional dedication produces fecundity of idea and action.

Pisces 20°-22½° *Leo:*

This segment generates true belief out of a will to believe. It approaches the self magically, with the idea that if it affirms its powers, then those powers exist. It questions itself to itself but does not like to be questioned by others. It loves others for whatever in them is completely unique or individualistic.

The love nature is enveloped in an aura of mysticism. This segment tends to personify its love in another human being. Sexual involvement is experienced almost purely as a token of complete and intimate union which is ultimately ineffable. It is strongly influenced by other people both positively and negatively, and therefore must develop sure mechanisms of defense to survive.

It either guards itself carefully against temptation or throws itself into it with complete abandon.

Loneliness is a common problem of this segment, because it tends to express itself in its own terms and from its own viewpoint. Often much energy is recycled back into the self in an attempt to rule the hidden and unconscious inner forces.

It needs to work out its own problems in its own way, so that it can feel that they have truly been worked out.

The Tarot: Pisces (The Martyr, #12) combines with Leo (The Sun, #21). to produce Venus (The Two Paths, #6). Hence, dedication becomes an act of will which burns the dross out of personality, leaving pure love.

Pisces 22½°-25° *Virgo:*

This segment believes that anything it feels to be true can be proven. It questions itself so that it can refine what it already knows. Belief comes before proof, but proof is an important means of checking and assuring the beliefs.

Its dedication manifests as dilligence. It wants to

work at seemingly insurmountable tasks and will accept projects where the odds of success are slim.

This segment's genius lies in its ability to bridge gaps in knowledge by means of faith, and lapses of faith by gaining more knowledge. This segment is good for nurses and doctors, because there is strong sympathy for anyone who is ill.

Much energy may be directed into trying to convince others of its beliefs, and also trying to convince itself. It accumulates knowledge through its attitude of inquiry into the validity of its credo.

This segment is the feminine principle in a state of complete dedication and submission. It desires to seek out its hidden gifts and talents and to refine them. If is often interested in occultism. Its genius lies in being able to use seeming limitations to its own benefit.

The Tarot: Pisces (The Martyr, #12) combines with Virgo (Veiled Isis, #2) to produce Taurus (The Alchemist, #14). Hence, dedication to exploring and researching the unseen is a means of achieving regeneration.

Pisces 25°-27½° *Libra:*

This segment is helpful, non-combative, and does not like to argue. It is sympathetic, but not condescending. By manifesting kindness in the face of negativity, it weakens selfishness. It is quick to compromise to maintain peace. All this often leads to being used by other people, but this segment is rarely aware of this, and so is unharmed by it. It often experiences difficulties in marriage, and it works out its karma through close personal ties. Often there is an over-pronounced feeling of being obligated to others.

Possibly in the light of past life involvements, this feeling of obligation is not as overblown as it may seem.

This segment is devoted in a quiet manner. Its giving-in is always on a material or lip-service basis. It never gives in psychologically. Its surface resiliance hides a core of stone. It displays a complete acceptance of the outward structure of reality as it sees it.

Often it associates with people who are extremely different from itself.

It is powerfully psychosomatic. Anything which it believes, it makes true. Others have a hard time getting through to it. When a thought is successfully planted in its mind by someone else, this thought has strong effect whether it be supportive or devastating.

The Tarot: Pisces (The Martyr, #12) combines with Libra (Isis Unveiled, #3) to produce Saturn (The Black Magician, #15). Hence, devotion springs from sympathy which is aware of the force of fatality, and subverts this force by refusing to fight it.

Pisces 27½°-30° *Scorpio:*

This segment knows that death is no end. It may even have a sensuous desire for death. Often it lacks ambition, but this is usually a positive trait in that it can relax and flow with any current in which it is caught.

It searches for a home and like Ulysses it must become resolved (Pisces, 12th house) to change (Scorpio, 8th house). It must accept what providence gives it before it can reach its goal. Often, though, this segment will leave home to force itself to experience reality on a broader basis. Home, in this context, must be taken as a place located in the mind, rather than in the world.

This segment weathers intensive personality changes with ease. Its core beliefs are unshakeable. It desires peace and manifests passive resistance in the face of disappointments. Its sexual nature is extremely sensitive.

It likes to lose itself in abstractions and the intangibles of the mind. It loves the act of going somewhere rather than arriving.

It enters trance states easily. Its problems are often overcome in sudden and unexpected ways, and it usually manifests a rebirth of strength and energy later in life.

The Tarot: Pisces (The Martyr, #12) combines with Scorpio (The Sovereign, #4) to produce Mars (The Lightning, #16). Hence, devotion, if it is pure, produces realization which can strike like lightning, granting self-perfection.

4 CHAPTER FOUR

TAROT RELATIONSHIPS TO DWADASHAMSAS

The following is a table of numerical additions of dwadashamsas as laid out in this book. The horizontal lines are the signs, and the vertical lines are the dwadashamsas of each sign in terms of their placement in that sign (1st, 2nd, 3rd, etc.). Beneath the square is a key on the meaning of the numbers in the square according to the Tarot.

SIGNS:	DWADS: 1st	2nd	3rd	4th	5th	6th	7th	8th	9th	10th	11th	12th
Aries:	17 (13+4)	20 (13+7)	21 (13+8)	22 (13+9)	7 (13+12)	8 (13+13)	9 (13+14)	3 (13+17)	4 (13+18)	5 (13+19)	15 (13+2)	16 (13+3)
Taurus:	17 (14+3)	18 (14+4)	21 (14+7)	22 (14+8)	5 (14+9)	8 (14+12)	9 (14+13)	10 (14+14)	4 (14+17)	5 (14+18)	6 (14+19)	16 (14+2)
Gemini:	19 (17+2)	20 (17+3)	21 (17+4)	6 (17+7)	7 (17+8)	8 (17+9)	11 (17+12)	3 (17+13)	4 (17+14)	7 (17+17)	8 (17+18)	9 (17+19)
Cancer:	10 (18+19)	20 (18+2)	21 (18+3)	22 (18+4)	7 (18+7)	8 (18+8)	9 (18+9)	3 (18+12)	4 (18+13)	5 (18+14)	8 (18+17)	9 (18+18)
Leo:	10 (19+18)	11 (19+19)	21 (19+2)	22 (19+3)	5 (19+4)	8 (19+7)	9 (19+8)	10 (19+9)	4 (19+12)	5 (19+13)	6 (19+14)	17 (19+17)
Virgo:	19 (2+17)	20 (2+18)	21 (2+19)	4 (2+2)	5 (2+3)	6 (2+4)	9 (2+7)	10 (2+8)	11 (2+9)	14 (2+12)	15 (2+13)	16 (2+14)
Libra:	17 (3+14)	20 (3+17)	21 (3+18)	22 (3+19)	5 (3+2)	6 (3+3)	7 (3+4)	10 (3+7)	11 (3+8)	12 (3+9)	15 (3+12)	16 (3+13)
Scorpio:	17 (4+13)	18 (4+14)	21 (4+17)	22 (4+18)	5 (4+19)	6 (4+2)	7 (4+3)	8 (4+4)	11 (4+7)	12 (4+8)	13 (4+9)	16 (4+12)
Sagittarius:	19 (7+12)	20 (7+13)	21 (7+14)	6 (7+17)	7 (7+18)	8 (7+19)	9 (7+2)	10 (7+3)	11 (7+4)	14 (7+7)	15 (7+8)	16 (7+9)
Capricorn:	17 (8+9)	20 (8+12)	21 (8+13)	22 (8+14)	5 (8+17)	8 (8+18)	9 (8+19)	10 (8+2)	11 (8+3)	12 (8+4)	15 (8+7)	16 (8+8)
Aquarius:	17 (9+8)	18 (9+9)	21 (9+12)	22 (9+13)	5 (9+14)	8 (9+17)	9 (9+18)	10 (9+19)	11 (9+2)	12 (9+3)	13 (9+4)	16 (9+7)
Pisces:	19 (12+7)	20 (12+8)	21 (12+9)	6 (12+12)	7 (12+13)	8 (12+14)	11 (12+17)	3 (12+18)	4 (12+19)	14 (12+2)	15 (12+3)	16 (12+4)

3—Isis Unveiled (Libra)
4—The Sovereign (Scorpio)
5—The Hierophant (Jupiter)
6—The Two Paths (Venus)
7—The Conquerer (Sagittarius)
8—The Balance (Capricorn)
9—The Sage (Aquarius)
10—The Wheel (Uranus)
11—The Enchantress (Neptune)
12—The Martyr (Pisces)
13—The Reaper (Aries)
14—The Alchemist (Taurus)
15—The Black Magician (Saturn)
16—The Lightning (Mars)
17—The Star (Gemini)
18—The Moon (Cancer)
19—The Sun (Leo)
20—The Sarcophagus (the Moon)
21—The Adept (the Sun)
22—The Materialist (Pluto)

(Note: Tarot cards numbered 18 and 19 are *called* "The Sun" and "The Moon," but they rule the signs Cancer and Leo respectively. Cards number 20 and 21 rule the heavenly bodies Sun and Moon).

The upper number in each square on the previous page represents the numerological value of the particular dwadashamsa in question. The number is obtained by adding the number of the sign to the number of the sub-ruler of the sign's particular dwadashamsa. The lower numbers in each square show this addition. Any number over 22 is reduced by adding its digits. This process is sometimes called "casting out nines," because it is the same as continuing to subtract nines from the number until this can be no longer done. In the case of the table though, the nines have been "cast out" only until a sum under 22 is reached. This is why the first dwadashamsa of Aries is shown as 17 rather than 8, (1 + 7).

The first dwadashamsa of each sign is associated with the twelfth house. It is like the first appearance of the sign, and the twelfth house is where any planet or sign first "appears" in the sky. The second dwadashamsa of each sign is associated with the eleventh house, the third with the tenth house, and so on.

The first dwadashamsa of a sign is associated with the numbers 17, 19, and 10, as can be seen from the table. Six signs have the number 17 associated with their first dwadashamsa, four signs have the number 19 associated with their first dwadashamsa, and two signs have 10 associated with their first dwadashamsa. Note that the four signs with the number 19 in their first dwadashamsa are the mutable signs, and that the signs which have the number 10 associated with their first dwadashamsa are the signs Cancer and Leo, special in that they are ruled by the Lights (Sun and Moon). This indicates that the first dwadashamsa of the mutable signs have to do with perfection and purification (twelfth house) of individuality, (Leo, the Adept, #19). The first dwadashamsa of the signs Cancer and Leo have to do with perfection and purification (twelfth house) of the creativity, (Uranus, The Wheel, #10). The rest of the first dwadashamsa of the signs have to do with perfection and purification (twelfth house) of faith, (Gemini, The Star, #17).

In the second column we find the numbers 11, 18, and 20. 11 is associated with the second dwadashamsa of Leo, the number 18 is associated with the second dwadashamsa of the other *fixed* signs, and 20 is associated with the second dwadashamsa of the cardinal and mutable signs. This shows that the second dwadashamsa correlates with force (Neptune, The Enchantress, #11) in Leo's case, mediumship (Cancer, The Moon, #18) in the case of the other fixed signs, and emotion, cycles, and timing (The Moon, The Sarcophagus, #20) in the case of the other signs. Since these are the second dwadashamsas of the signs, they are associated with the eleventh house, which esoterically symbolizes the qualification of energy, or in other words, how we manifest something that we have — what we do with it. As mentioned in the introductory essay on astro-numerology, the eleventh house is esoterically associated with the sign Libra, and the number three — activity, dynamism, fruitfulness.

Hopefully this chart will stimulate the student to see more clearly the underlying pattern of the dwadashamsas. The third, fourth, and fifth, etc. dwadashamsa of the signs can be analyzed in much the same was as the first two, and as one continues to think about the chart, more and more innerconnections will be seen.

An extremely important aspect about this chart is the manner in which the signs combine. If we compute all the possible sign pairings, we will find that they are seventy-eight in number.* This includes doublings, such as pairing Leo with Leo. Now if we take any pair, such as Virgo and Scorpio, we see that Virgo rules the sixth dwadashamsa of Scorpio, and that Scorpio rules the sixth dwadashamsa of Virgo. Hence, Virgo and Scorpio have a seventh house relationship. (The sixth dwadashamsa of all the signs is associated with the seventh house). This shows that purification (Virgo) co-ordinated with realization (Scorpio) is a function of the seventh house — the house ruled by Aquarius in the esoteric system and associated with the growth and development of wisdom.

All other sign combinations can be analyzed in this manner, and this will provide a better understanding of how signs combine, and hence a better understanding of the nature of the signs themselves.

The analyses of this chart are certainly not in depth, but they point the way to further study, and an idea of how the student can further understand the zodiac.

*There are seventy-eight cards in the traditional tarot deck!

APPENDIX

RELATING DWADASHAMSAS TO BIRTHDATES

This book can be useful even to the novice of Astrology. Just by knowing the birthdate of an individual, the degree of that person's Sun can be easily approximated and hence correlated to a dwadashamsa. The following is a list of dates, and the degrees (dwadashamsas) that correlate to these dates. Bear in mind that these degrees (dwadashamsas) relate only to a person's Sun; the positions of the other planets will require the use of an ephemeris for that birthdate. Also bear in mind that these birthdates, relating to degrees of an individual's Sun, are approximate: they are close, but may be off by <u>one</u> dwadashamsa, due to the <u>time</u> of birth, and also due to the Earth's movement around the Sun—a movement which is fairly consistent every year, but not exactly the same from one year to the next (about six hours off per year according to our calendar, hence the "leap year" every fourth year to make up the "lost" 24-hour day over the four-year period).

DATE		SUN'S DEGREE	
March	21-23	**Aries**	0-2½
"	23-26	"	2½-5
"	26-28	"	5-7½
"	28-31	"	7½-10
April	1-2	"	10-12½
"	2-5	"	12½-15
"	5-7	"	15-17½
"	7-10	"	17½-20
"	10-12	"	20-22½
"	12-15	"	22½-25
"	15-17	"	25-27½
"	17-20	"	27½-30

DATE		SUN'S DEGREE	
"	20-23	**Taurus**	0-2½
"	23-25	"	2½-5
"	25-28	"	5-7½
"	28-30	"	7½-10
May	1-3	"	10-12½
"	3-6	"	12½-15
"	6-8	"	15-17½
"	8-11	"	17½-20
"	11-13	"	20-22½
"	13-16	"	22½-25
"	16-19	"	25-27½
"	19-21	"	27½-30
"	21-24	**Gemini**	0-2½
"	24-26	"	2½-5
"	26-29	"	5-7½
"	29-30	"	7½-10
June	1-3	"	10-12½
"	3-6	"	12½-15
"	6-8	"	15-17½
"	8-11	"	17½-20
"	11-14	"	20-22½
"	14-16	"	22½-25
"	16-19	"	25-27½
"	19-21	"	27½-30
"	21-24	**Cancer**	0-2½
"	24-27	"	2½-5
"	27-29	"	5-7½
"	2-**July** 2	"	7½-10
July	2-4	"	10-12½
"	4-7	"	12½-15
"	7-10	"	15-17½
"	10-12	"	17½-20
"	12-15	"	20-22½
"	15-18	"	22½-25
"	18-20	"	25-27½
"	20-23	"	27½-30

DATE	SUN'S DEGREE
" 23-25	**Leo** 0-2½
" 25-28	" 2½-5
" 28-31	" 5-7½
August 1-2	" 7½-10
" 2-5	" 10-12½
" 5-8	" 12½-15
" 8-10	" 15-17½
" 10-13	" 17½-20
" 13-15	" 20-22½
" 15-18	" 22½-25
" 18-20	" 25-27½
" 20-23	" 27½-30
" 23-26	**Virgo** 0-2½
" 26-28	" 2½-5
" 28-31	" 5-7½
Aug. 31-**Sept.** 3	" 7½-10
September 3-5	" 10-12½
" 5-8	" 12½-15
" 8-10	" 15-17½
" 10-13	" 17½-20
" 13-15	" 20-22½
" 15-18	" 22½-25
" 18-20	" 25-27½
" 20-23	" 27½-30
" 23-26	**Libra** 0-2½
" 26-28	" 2½-5
" 28-**Oct.** 1	" 5-7½
October 1-3	" 7½-10
" 3-6	" 10-12½
" 6-8	" 12½-15
" 8-11	" 15-17½
" 11-13	" 17½-20
" 13-16	" 20-22½
" 16-18	" 22½-25
" 18-21	" 25-27½
" 21-23	" 27½-30

187

DATE		SUN'S DEGREE	
"	23-26	Scorpio	0-2½
"	26-28	"	2½-5
"	28-31	"	5-7½
November	1-3	"	7½-10
"	3-5	"	10-12½
"	5-7	"	12½-15
"	7-10	"	15-17½
"	10-12	"	17½-20
"	12-15	"	20-22½
"	15-17	"	22½-25
"	17-20	"	25-27½
"	20-22	"	27½-30
"	22-25	Sagittarius	0-2½
"	25-27	"	2½-5
"	27-30	"	5-7½
Nov. 30-Dec. 2		"	7½-10
December	2-5	"	10-12½
"	5-7	"	12½-15
"	7-9	"	15-17½
"	9-12	"	17½-20
"	12-14	"	20-22½
"	14-17	"	22½-25
"	17-19	"	25-27½
"	19-22	"	27½-30
"	22-24	Capricorn	0-2½
"	24-27	"	2½-5
"	27-29	"	5-7½
"	29-Jan. 1	"	7½-10
January	1-3	"	10-12½
"	3-6	"	12½-15
"	6-8	"	15-17½
"	8-11	"	17½-20
"	11-13	"	20-22½
"	13-15	"	22½-25
"	15-18	"	25-27½
"	18-20	"	27½-30

DATE		SUN'S DEGREE	
''	20-23	**Aquarius**	0-2½
''	23-25	''	2½-5
''	25-28	''	5-7½
''	28-30	''	7½-10
Jan. 30-**Feb.** 1		''	10-12½
February	1-4	''	12½-15
''	4-6	''	15-17½
''	6-9	''	17½-20
''	9-11	''	20-22½
''	11-14	''	22½-25
''	14-16	''	25-27½
''	16-19	''	27½-30
''	19-21	**Pisces**	0-2½
''	21-24	''	2½-5
''	24-26	''	5-7½
''	26-**March** 1	''	7½-10
March	1-3	''	10-12½
''	3-6	''	12½-15
''	6-8	''	15-17½
''	8-11	''	17½-20
''	11-13	''	20-22½
''	13-16	''	22½-25
''	16-18	''	25-27½
''	18-21	''	27½-30

HOW TO USE THIS APPENDIX:

1. Find out birthdate of person.
2. Locate birthdate in these tables.
3. Determine which degrees (dwadashamsa) relate to this birthdate, and by looking upwards in the columns, also determine which sign these degrees pertain to.
4. Look up this degree segment in Chapter Three of this book.

Example: John Doe is born October 5th. What dwadashamsa is his Sun located in?

According to the tables of this appendix, October 5th correlates to 10-12½ degrees. As we look up the column marked SUN'S DEGREE, we first come to the sign of Libra. Therefore John Doe's Sun is located in approximately 10-12½ degrees of Libra.

Turning to Chapter Three, we will find this segment of Libra described on page 115, where it is identified as the Gemini dwad of the sign Libra. The description therein should bear recognizable resemblance to a part of John Doe's nature, assuming that on October 5th, the Sun's degree was posited between 10-12½ degrees of Libra (which is most likely true).

In many cases there will be an overlap in this appendix. For example, a person born October 6th may have his Sun in either the 10-12½ degree segment of Libra, or the 12½-15 degree segment. Without an accurate horoscope, constructed from the location of birth as well as the time of birth, it is impossible to be certain which is the correct dwadashamsa. However, even without an accurately constructed horoscope, one of these two descriptions should bear remarkable likeness to the person under study, and hence helpful insight into the understanding of that person should result. 190